THE **ALPHABET** OF **POWERFUL EXISTENCE**

an A-Z guide to well-being, wisdom and worthiness

by
Olga Sheean

Published by InsideOut Media

Cover design and layout by Lewis Evans
lewis@lewisevans.net

ISBN 978-0-9879291-2-9

CONTENTS

INTRODUCTION

Fifty-two weeks of inspiration and empowerment

This book is a compilation of 26 transformative twosomes that are complementary and interdependent. Mastering one enables you to more easily master the other; and mastering them all enables you to live a much more powerful, magical, fulfilling life.

Altogether, there are 52 themes; if you read and practise one for every week of the year, you will discover aspects of you – and of the universe – that you never knew existed.

Many of these themes (such as acceptance, trust, self-expression and validation) refer to what I call our 'missing pieces' – essential formative qualities that we needed to have cultivated in us as children, in order to be complete, but failed to get from our parents/teachers/caregivers. As a result, many of these qualities are not a natural part of us and, when we lack any of them, we become distorted and tend to make compromises in the hope of getting the acceptance, respect etc that has been missing. We also come to certain negative subconscious conclusions about our worth – often believing ourselves to be unimportant, unacceptable, unlovable or not good enough, as a result.

Your mind is your magnet... make it work for you!

Our subconscious mind is very magnetic, always attracting to us whatever we need in order to discover, heal, express and empower ourselves, in accordance with how it has been programmed. Our missing pieces represent a key element of our early programming, and they have a powerful impact on the nature and quality of our lives. They cause us to attract people and situations in which these same qualities are also missing, which means that our partners, friends or colleagues are usually unable to give us the very things we most want from them. This usually results in conflict, heartache and frustration, unless we understand how things work, deep in our subconscious. The key to resolving these issues is to mindfully fill in our missing pieces in practical ways so that the missing qualities become a natural, instinctive part of us and of our lives. By demonstrating and cultivating the very qualities that we seek, we positively reprogram our subconscious minds to work powerfully and positively in our favour.

Fill in your missing pieces so you become more complete

Think about your life. What qualities are missing or deficient in your relationships, work and/ or personal life? They may include trust, respect, validation or intimacy. Or they might be self-expression, honesty or connection. Whatever qualities you identify are YOUR missing pieces, even if they appear to only be missing in others and not in you.

Your missing pieces show up in different ways, and it's often difficult for you to identify how they block you or manifest in your life. You can much more readily see what's missing in others, and once you realize that those close to you represent a reflection of what's missing in you (as

1

well as what's wonderful about you), you can begin the work of filling in your own missing pieces – which is the most powerful and effective way to make your life work beautifully.

The more you practise and demonstrate whatever qualities may have been missing in your relationships, work or personal life, the more you start to attract those qualities in your partners, colleagues, clients and friends. The key to making your life complete, therefore, lies in making yourself complete from the inside out, in as many practical, everyday ways as you can. As you do this, you automatically attract whatever has been missing in your life – and whatever works best for you, even if you don't yet know what that is.

This book is a simple guide to making you complete; the more you use it, the deeper you go inside yourself, and the richer, more complete and more fulfilling your life becomes.

As you do the all-important work of empowering you, remember that your missing pieces:

- determine what circumstances and people you attract;
- cause you to attract partners with the same missing pieces as you;
- distort/diminish your sense of self, creating insecurity and doubts;
- leave you with certain faculties undeveloped or unexpressed;
- bring you challenges designed to strengthen/heal the aspects of you made wobbly by early negative programming;
- are part of a subconscious program relating to your life's path;
- are designed to show you where your true personal power lies;
- represent the flip side of your greatest strengths.

Your missing pieces hold the key to having the life you want. When you fill in your missing pieces in practical ways, you start living life on your terms. By making you #1 in your life, by saying no to whatever doesn't work for you, and by generally demonstrating healthy self-worth, self-respect and self-acceptance, your world starts to revolve around you, rather than you being a reaction to your circumstances. Things start to work and magic starts to happen. The more you do this, the more things fall into place in accordance with what is best for you, and the easier life becomes. Things start to flow; people start to support you; new opportunities open up; and you start to attract more positive, loving, fulfilling dynamics in your life. You are effectively reprogramming your subconscious mind, which is the most powerful, magnetic part of you and has more control over your life than you can possibly imagine. As you positively reprogram it, by filling in your missing pieces, you begin to realize that you have the power to change your circumstances, to heal your relationships and to thrive in every area of your life.

This process inevitably takes you on a journey of self-discovery, healing and personal empowerment, introducing you to parts of yourself that you never knew existed, and making your life more dynamic and fulfilling than you could ever have imagined. It will also put you in touch with your passions, creativity and greatest strengths, showing you the power and impact of being uniquely, fully, unflinchingly you.

A

acceptance
& authenticity

acceptance

*the act of taking/receiving something offered [**such as your uniqueness**]; favourable reception/approval [**of yourself and all that you are/can be**]; the act of assenting [**giving yourself permission to be fully you**] or believing in something [**such as the power of you**]*

Why is it important?

- Acceptance is a vital human nutrient—as essential to humans as water is to a plant.
- Accepting ourselves for who we are is the key to a dynamic, fulfilling and joyful life.
- The more we accept ourselves unconditionally, the more everyone else does, too.
- It's needed more than anything else on Earth to restore our natural balance.
- Healthy self-acceptance enables us to live the rich, magical lives we're meant to live.
- We need it for our health, well-being, sanity, sense of purpose, success and happiness.
- We need it for harmony, collaboration, community ...and our survival as a species.

*As you generate greater acceptance on the inside,
you begin to see magic happening on the outside.*

What's the problem?

- It's been chronically deficient in our mental, spiritual and emotional diet for centuries.
- It's the #1 'missing piece' in our makeup, causing insecurities and self-doubt.
- Trying to gain acceptance from others (as we all do) comes from low self-worth.
- Our neediness around acceptance/approval pushes away the very things we want.
- This need leads to unhealthy compromises that bring us more of what we don't want.
- We need to be accepting of ourselves, rather than trying to be accepted by others.
- We may have difficulty fully, truly loving, trusting or respecting ourselves or others.
- When we lack healthy self-acceptance, it's hard to say NO.

Without self-acceptance, it's hard to fully be yourself, express yourself or even know yourself.

How can you fix it?

You can practise and demonstrate healthy self-acceptance by:

- putting yourself first, in healthy ways, every single day
- eating good food, resting and taking time out for friendships and creative activities
- making healthy boundaries and saying NO to whatever doesn't work for you
- avoiding compromises or choices that don't feel right for you
- expressing your opinion, feelings and sense of humour, regardless of others' reactions
- expressing yourself creatively, in how you dress, through music, art, your unique gifts
- loving yourself unconditionally, in the face of any rejection, criticism or abuse.

With healthy self-acceptance, you are free to be powerfully, lovingly, creatively you —which brings you to authenticity.

A acceptance & authenticity

authenticity

the quality/condition of being authentic, trustworthy or genuine [being uniquely, quirkily you]

Why is it important?

- Authenticity is the purest expression of who we are.
- Being authentic brings depth and meaning to our relationships.
- It has a powerful impact on others, encouraging them to be equally honest and open.
- Anything less than authenticity is really a lie–a contrived or learned way of operating.
- Striving to impress others fails to make our hearts sing (or our lives work).
- Being true to self in word/action/intention is the only way to get the fulfillment we seek.
- Authenticity promotes contentment, spontaneity, vulnerability and openness.
- It also engenders emotional freedom and the ability to genuinely love.

There is nothing more rewarding than exploring, expressing and sharing your true self.

What's the problem?

- We're afraid to be ourselves, for fear of rejection or ridicule.
- We've been taught to relate, behave or perform in ways that impress others.
- Our face-paced world makes it difficult to find presence of mind.
- Without that presence, we cannot fully connect with our deeper thoughts or feelings.
- The pressure to perform and succeed prevents us from being more honest and open.
- Being authentic takes work; it requires perpetual monitoring of our feelings.
- It means ensuring that our thoughts, words and actions are based on heartfelt sincerity.
- If we're not behaving in accordance with our heart, we're not being authentic.

Anything less than authenticity is a compromise— the foundation of mediocrity.

How can you fix it?

You can practise and demonstrate authenticity by:

- maintaining friendships only with those who love and support you in healthy ways
- pursuing a line of work that has meaning for you
- speaking and acting with honesty and integrity, regardless of the expected outcome
- remembering that speaking out enables you to hear the truth or power of what you say
- being honest and sincere with yourself regarding your motivations
- making decisions out of choice, rather than fear
- spontaneously showing and expressing your emotions in the moment
- speaking your mind, based on self-acceptance rather than self-aggrandizement
- being as you are in the moment, versus pretending to be something you're not
- sharing yourself honestly, openly and freely with others.

Your ideal partner will only want the real you.

B boundaries & balance

boundaries

*the limits we set in relationships to protect ourselves and to let others know what is acceptable and unacceptable to us [**saying no to whatever doesn't feel right or healthy for us**]*

Why are they important?

- Personal boundaries define us, indicating our likes/dislikes, values and self-worth.
- They also determine how closely we allow others to approach.
- Having solid boundaries is essential for physical and emotional health.
- The boundaries we make are determined by our beliefs, feelings and experiences.
- Boundaries define our value, our self-respect and how far we allow others to push us.
- Healthy boundaries protect us from disrespect, exploitation, manipulation and abuse.
- Having healthy boundaries is crucial in any relationship, so we retain our sense of self.
- Healthy boundaries set us up for a more balanced and fulfilling life.

Saying NO to what doesn't work for us automatically attracts something better.

What's the problem?

- If we have low self-esteem, it's hard to assert ourselves/make healthy boundaries.
- We need a strong sense of self to know when/where to make appropriate boundaries.
- We may not know what a healthy boundary is, or even what constitutes abuse.
- Negative personal experiences affect our ability to make healthy boundaries.
- If we have mushy boundaries, we're unclear about what to let in and what to keep out.
- A lack of healthy boundaries usually results in co-dependence and some form of abuse.
- Not having good boundaries can also lead to regrets and self-recrimination.
- If our boundaries are too rigid, we may keep others at a distance, resulting in isolation.

The boundaries we make tell people
how they should treat us.

How can you fix it?

You can practise making healthy boundaries by:

- saying NO to whatever doesn't work for you
- making choices based on what feels best for you
- standing up for yourself when something doesn't feel right
- rejecting any form of abuse—insults, verbal/physical/sexual harassment or aggression
- not being a doormat or catering to the needs of others at the expense of your own
- clearly defining your personal space/belongings, while respecting others'
- leaving an abusive/unhealthy relationship after you've said NO to it
- taking responsibility for your own life and not taking responsibility for other people's
- behaving respectfully towards others, even if they are not respectful towards you.

You empower, impress and uplift yourself with every
healthy boundary you make,
which takes you to a place of balance.

B boundaries & balance

balance

*a state of equilibrium or equipoise; mental steadiness or emotional stability; habit of calm behaviour, judgement and/or priorities [**a healthy mix and prioritization of all the things that matter most in life**]*

Why is it important?

- A healthy balance in life is the key to a healthy body and mind—and vice versa.
- Respecting our body's needs helps us keep things in perspective.
- Finding balance in our thoughts and emotions helps keep us happy and on track.
- To live well and long, we need balance in our diet, lifestyle, work and relationships.
- Without it, we may fall into ill-health or stress ...and may sometimes fall out of love.
- Balance brings clarity, which brings greater focus and easier/healthier decision-making.
- Making choices based on what's best for us helps us determine our true priorities.

*We know we've got the balance right
when everything works and flows smoothly.*

What's the problem?

- We're programmed to perform and succeed, versus going with what feels right.
- Competing demands on our time and energy throw us off balance and lead to stress.
- We rarely listen to our bodies until something goes wrong.
- Worries about money/survival/competence can cause us to do too much–or too little.
- We often compromise our needs in the hope of acceptance, recognition or reward.
- We're bombarded with information and messages that can cloud our vision and focus.
- Our numerous connections through electronic devices disconnect us from ourselves.

Losing our balance
can leave us battered and bruised.

How can you fix it?

You can regain a healthy balance in life by:

- Mindfully assessing what's important to you at home, at work and in relationships.
- Making time for friendships, exercise, relaxation and quiet reflection.
- Maintaining a healthy routine for meals and stress-free digestion.
- Allowing your body and intuition to guide your choices and commitments.
- Setting aside time to connect with your partner and nurture your relationship.
- Saying NO to friendships, contacts, activities or conversations that sap your energy.
- Creating clarity and focus by de-cluttering your home, your agenda and your mind.
- Delegating any non-essential activities so that you have more free time for you.
- Exploring creative exchanges with others–for support and community engagement.

When you're balanced, you're not on a tightrope or
heading for the safety net.
You're flying high with the greatest of ease.

C commitment & community

commitment

*the state of being committed or pledged [**to being the best you can be**]; an obligation or promise that restricts one's freedom [**but only if you commit to someone other than you**]*

Why is it important?

- Commitment to self is the most powerful kind of commitment you can make.
- It's about being fully you and being the best you can be, in all that you do.
- Healthy commitment means being dedicated to your personal evolution and growth.
- Being committed to self means making your health and your personal needs a priority.
- True commitment inspires action, dedication and fulfillment.
- Healthy commitment to what's best for you inspires healthy commitment in others.
- Commitment is the fuel we use to overcome objections, obstacles and doubts.

Commitment to self is the only kind of commitment that makes life worth living.

What's the problem?

- We're taught to commit to others or to some other person's agenda.
- If we're committed to others, we end up taking responsibility for them.
- Having no control over others, it makes no sense to commit to their agenda.
- Being committed to someone else (and not you) creates unhealthy dynamics.
- We often confuse commitment in a relationship with a fear of moving on.
- We don't realize that healthy commitment is a matter of free choice.
- If you're not fully committed to yourself, you're unlikely to ever get what you want.

If you commit to another person's agenda,
you probably have a hidden agenda of your own.

How can you fix it?

You can practise greater commitment to yourself by:

- doing what's best for your personal growth and fulfillment
- holding out for what you really want, despite any fears around not getting it
- finding the discipline and doing the work involved in getting the results you want
- standing up for your values and staying on track with your goals
- making your health a top priority, knowing that you can't negotiate with your body
- staying committed to what's right for you, so you can be fully committed in love
- actively exploring ways to be more expressive, creative and fulfilled
- taking action to realize your dreams and creative projects
- getting whatever support you need to stay on track with your goals
- not allowing other people's demands/objections to stop you from moving ahead.

Actively committing to you is best for you
—and for your community.

C commitment & community

community

a social group residing in a specific locality, sharing government and often having a common cultural/historical heritage; a sense of belonging/involvement and meaningful connection

Why is it important?

- Having a sense of belonging is an integral part of being human.
- As social animals with a history of tribal systems, we're innately drawn to others.
- As individuals, we can all contribute something; collectively, we can do even more.
- Having interactive communities helps us to evolve as individuals and as a society.
- A cohesive community represents an important bank of resources, skills and capital.
- We grow through sharing ourselves and supporting each other; we're better people.
- Community helps us to interact in more generous, considerate and loving ways.
- As our cities expand, we need community more than ever before.

Having a sense of community
is what binds and supports us,
inspiring us to show up and share.

13

What's the problem?

- With our fast-paced living, we're becoming more disconnected from each other.
- Although we may share a building or a street, we rarely know our neighbours.
- Technology has us connecting virtually more than in person.
- Despite our vast numbers, many of us are desperately lonely and alone.
- A lack of community can lead to depression, social isolation and suicides.
- We need meaningful interaction to foster greater tolerance and understanding.
- We lack the deep sense of tribal alliance that nourishes us emotionally.
- We experience more stress if we fail to satisfy our natural urge to socially engage.
- Actively engaging in our community can give us a healthy sense of purpose.

Without a sense of belonging,
we can feel lonely, even in a crowd,
and useless, even in a world that needs us.

How can you fix it?

You can cultivate a healthy sense of community and belonging by:

- contributing your time, skills or other resources to your local community
- offering your services or even just warm words and a smile to those in need
- signing up for a night class or workshop with like-minded locals
- volunteering at your local MP's office
- joining local meet-ups, fruit-picking events and other local initiatives
- participating in local debates about local issues
- becoming a Big Brother/Sister and sharing your wisdom with a special young person.

Getting involved in your community is like
suddenly finding a whole new family.

D determination & daring

determination

*firmness of purpose [**unwavering, focused and hell-bent on getting there**], a resolve to achieve something and a refusal to give up, no matter how tough things might get*

Why is it important?

- Determination has power, often opening doors that might otherwise stay closed.
- Committing to something builds character, optimism and a sense of purpose.
- Being determined, in the face of challenges or doubt, builds confidence and courage.
- We're far more likely to achieve our goals if we are determined to do so.
- Being determined has a positive effect on others, inspiring them to be equally so.
- It's extremely gratifying when we achieve something that was challenging to do.

*Be determined to succeed, on your terms,
rather than allowing your success
to be determined by others.*

What's the problem?

- Since we all have self-doubts and fears, we often give up too easily.

- There's a lot of competition ...and we don't realize it's just a test of our conviction in self.

- It's easy to convince ourselves that something won't work, if we haven't done it yet.

- Not everyone believes they have the courage, will power or skills to succeed.

- Not everyone believes that they deserve to be successful.

- If we dwell in negativity, we're unlikely to feel very determined to succeed.

- Stress and emotional upsets/insecurities can weaken our resolve.

If you're determined to make a difference,
you will.

How can you fix it?

You can cultivate greater determination by:

- asking for help or support to keep you positive and on track

- not letting your emotions/insecurities/doubts weaken your resolve

- staying active and engaged so you stay energized and upbeat

- encouraging yourself with positive self-talk any time doubts creep in

- mixing with others who support your vision or goals

- regularly acknowledging/making a list of all that you've achieved so far

- joining a mastermind group to create accountability for yourself

- focusing on what you love about what you're doing, to keep the passion/vision alive

- reminding yourself of all the emotional/financial/physical payoffs from succeeding.

The more you do, the more you can do, and the more
daring you become.

D determination & daring

daring

seeking out and/or being willing to do things that involve risk or danger [such as being daringly, outrageously you]; bold, brave and adventurous [because life is meant to be lived!]

Why is it important?

- Doing anything new, worthwhile or cutting-edge requires taking some risks.
- Only by taking risks can we discover what's possible and what we're made of.
- Being daring requires a solid faith in self, which is a magnet for good things.
- Avoiding all risks creates a life of routine, mediocrity and unfulfilled dreams.
- When we're daring, we can see opportunities where others see only problems.
- Being daring generates respect and admiration in others; it's contagious!
- If we dare to initiate something big, we often inspire others to come on board.
- Being daring means acting in spite of what others might think, say or do.
- Being daring means being you–uncompromisingly.

Daring to excel is the same thing as daring to be you.

What's the problem?

- We must overcome our own fears/doubts in order to act boldly.
- We've been taught to play safe, not to be powerful.
- Our desire for safety and easy solutions leads to unhealthy compromises.
- We often let others' criticisms/doubts/objections undermine our urge to be bold.
- People fear failing, not realizing that not risking failure is not an achievement.
- Being afraid of rejection or ridicule stops us from taking risks.
- We often confuse being daring with being reckless.

*Nothing significant ever really changes
unless you dare to do something significant.*

How can you fix it?

You can become more daring by:

- never thinking in terms of failure–even if you seem to not succeed
- not allowing others to feed your fears or diminish your commitment
- asking for what you want, which greatly assists you in getting it
- being boldly proactive rather than waiting for things to come to you
- remembering how exciting it is to be around daring people (like you)
- expressing your opinions, feelings and values with those of like mind
- acting boldly, even if you don't yet feel very daring
- reminding yourself that daring people create their own success.

*You dare because you care about you and me.
In daring, you are sharing you with me.*

E emotionality & evolution

emotionality

the quality or state of being emotionally responsive; emotional nature or quality

Why is it important?

- Having emotions is what makes us human and distinguishes us from animals.
- Our emotions have a profound impact on our mental and physical health.
- Emotions give meaning and significance to our lives; they make us care.
- They affect our thinking, our behaviour and our intentions.
- Positive emotions can motivate us to take positive, life-enhancing actions.
- Our emotions can help channel our energies into resolving life's challenges.
- Emotions such as fear can help keep us safe by causing us to avoid or flee danger.
- Our emotional intelligence plays a key role in our decision-making.
- Expressing ourselves emotionally enables us to understand each other better.

Emotional honesty is our most powerful faculty.

What's the problem?

- We're rarely taught how to process or manage our emotions in healthy ways.
- Emotional pain/dysfunction gets handed down from generation to generation.
- We cannot have healthy relationships unless we're emotionally healthy.
- Unresolved negative emotions can lead to denial, depression, violence and abuse.
- Our modern diet and lifestyle have a huge impact on our emotions.
- If we're emotionally upset, we can make decisions that we later regret.
- Prolonged or excessive emotional instability can lead to mental illness.
- Being unable to resolve our emotions can result in isolation and withdrawal.
- Unhealthy emotions can distort our view of life, creating unhappiness.

Emotional dysfunction
is at the root of almost all our problems.

How can you fix it?

You can cultivate healthier emotionality by:

- finding ways to get emotionally present and connected (through music, nature...)
- allowing yourself to express your feelings in healthy ways
- getting whatever support you need to resolve any emotional pain, shame or angst
- sharing your feelings with others so you gain perspective or feedback
- acknowledging what you're feeling, rather than pushing it aside or discounting it
- staying physically active, engaged and healthy, to support your heart, body and mind
- allowing yourself to connect with others in heartfelt, meaningful ways
- daring to talk about what really matters to you, regardless of convention.

Your emotions take you where you're meant to go,
pushing you to grow and evolve.

E

emotionality & evolution

evolution

*the gradual, progressive change or development of something [**a human**], especially from a simple to a more complex form [**bringing greater self-awareness, creativity and self-mastery**]; any process of growth [**that enhances relationships, health, personal power and fulfillment**]*

Why is it important?

- Evolving is what we're designed to do, as human beings.
- We are always striving for more knowledge and better ways of doing things.
- We are driven to succeed and thrive, which pushes us to understand ourselves better.
- Striving to grow and to be our very best benefits everyone around us.
- Evolving emotionally, spiritually and mentally deepens our experience of life.
- Evolving means being creative in our thinking, our goals and our decisions.
- Being creative helps us to manifest what we want in life.
- Creativity is our primary way of evolving, innovating, inventing and problem-solving.

Creativity is what happens when we put aside our logical minds and allow ourselves to play.

21

What's the problem?

- We tend to favour practicalities over creative thinking or activities.
- Creativity is largely seen as a hobby, rather than an integral part of our makeup.
- Not growing or being open to change keeps us stuck in old patterns.
- Creativity is the key to the survival of individuals, companies and the human species.
- A lack of meaningful growth may cause us to compensate with food, alcohol, etc.
- We often think self-improvement means having more money or success.
- If we don't consciously grow and evolve, our relationships suffer.
- If we don't seek to know or understand ourselves, we're unlikely to get what we want.

If we always need to dwell in certainty,
we'll never evolve or experience
the freedom of creative thought.

How can you fix it?

You can enhance your creative evolution and growth by:

- exploring creative activities such as dance, acting, comedy and storytelling
- interacting with other creative thinkers, speakers and doers
- questioning everything, including your most cherished beliefs
- pushing yourself outside your limit/routine to experience something new
- always seeking to learn and to expand your mind, for greater fulfillment
- allowing yourself plenty of downtime for creative ideas to emerge and evolve
- continually re-assessing your priorities so you stay focused on what matters most
- engaging in work/friendships/activities that uplift, inspire and challenge you.

Furthering your personal evolution
is your most important mission in life.

F focus & fulfillment

focus

*the state of maximum distinctness or clarity of an image [**or your self-image**]; a centre of interest or activity [**you**]; a condition in which something can be clearly perceived [**who you really are**]; close or narrow attention/concentration [**on what matters**]*

Why is it important?

- Focusing on what we want helps us to get clear about how best to achieve it.
- When we are focused, we have more motivation and a clearer sense of purpose.
- With so much coming at us from all kinds of media, we need to be focused to succeed.
- If we're creative, with lots of ideas, it's essential to be focused so we follow through.
- We all multi-task and juggle priorities, which makes focus all the more important.
- Focusing on one or two things can be more productive than working harder on lots.
- By focusing our energies on one goal, we draw more life and energy to that objective.

What we focus on is what we get.

What's the problem?

- Without a healthy focus, our energies get dispersed and diffused.
- Focusing on too many things usually generates mixed results in all of them.
- We can easily be thrown off course by e-mails, social media, Internet browsing, etc.
- Too much multi-tasking prevents us from being focused and centred.
- Multi-tasking overloads the brain's processing capacity, with long-term effects.
- Chronic multi-tasking reduces productivity, memory and efficiency.
- It also reduces our ability to filter ideas and to do things properly or well.
- Trying to do too much creates stress, frustration and mental/emotional overload.

*If we don't focus,
everything gets a bit blurry.*

How can you fix it?

You can become more focused by:

- practising doing one thing at a time and doing it well
- reducing clutter and distractions from your home and workspace
- starting each day with a short list of what's most important and sticking to it
- checking e-mails/texts only a few times a day, at certain scheduled times
- breaking down tasks and goals into simple, practical steps
- scheduling certain times for meetings/interactions and keeping the rest for you
- organizing your daily routine with designated time for meals, relaxation and work
- respecting your own (and others') time frames and boundaries.

*When you focus on your feelings, your passion and your
goals, you find clarity, purpose and fulfillment.*

F

focus
& fulfillment

fulfillment

*satisfaction/happiness as a result of fully developing your abilities, character or potential; the achievement or realization of something desired/promised [**such as the realization of self**]*

Why is it important?

- Finding fulfillment through our personal achievements makes life worthwhile.
- Personal fulfillment is about achieving personal life goals that matter to the individual.
- Fulfillment brings happiness and satisfaction, which matters more than success.
- Fulfilling our potential is likely to be more rewarding than anything else.
- Fulfillment is more than a fleeting emotion; it's about living a meaningful life.
- It's a deep and lasting sense of accomplishment and purposeful direction.
- It's the personal, emotional reward/payoff we experience from our efforts.

It's not just doing things that brings fulfillment,
it's loving what we do.

What's the problem?

- We often lack fulfillment because we're not in touch with our purpose or true calling.
- A lack of fulfillment can drain our energy, motivation and sense of value.
- It can result in boredom, disinterest and emotional withdrawal.
- It can cause us to wish away our time, work on autopilot and not enjoy the present.
- Feeling unfulfilled causes stress and can affect our health and well-being.
- If we're unfulfilled, we may become argumentative, resentful or jealous of others.
- We may seek comfort in food/sex/drugs to distract ourselves from what's missing.

If we're unfulfilled,
we're not living the full life we're meant to live.

How can you fix it?

You can generate greater fulfillment by:

- acknowledging what areas of your life need to be re-assessed and adjusted
- making changes where you know changes need to be made, despite your fears
- paying attention to the small things, so you start to appreciate being alive
- identifying what doesn't feel right in your life and daring to make positive changes
- sharing your feelings with partner/friends for meaningful feedback
- really listening to others and being fully present in all your interactions
- focusing on the parts of your life that feel good and allowing them to inspire you
- staying honest with yourself about what you really want and what feels right
- allowing your feelings, passions and intuition to guide your choices and decisions.

The more fulfilled you become,
the more powerful your impact on the world.

G gratitude
& generosity

gratitude

*the quality of being thankful [**for your life, for others and for all that you are/can do**]; appreciation for, and readiness to return, kindness [**towards others and yourself**]*

Why is it important?

- Being grateful infuses our bodies with positive energy and well-being.
- It lowers our blood pressure, reduces stress and boosts our immune system.
- Perpetual gratitude makes us joyful and optimistic.
- It helps us to focus on the good things, which generates more of the same.
- It makes us more generous, compassionate and outgoing.
- When we're grateful, we feel worthy and we allow ourselves to receive.
- With gratitude, we expect good things to happen—and they do.

*When we're grateful for our greatness,
we're a powerful force for good.*

What's the problem?

- We often focus on our problems and on what's going wrong in our lives.
- The more negative we are, the less grateful we feel and the more we blame others.
- We focus more on getting what we want than on the joy of giving to others.
- Being consistently grateful requires conscious effort and mindful awareness.
- Gratitude should come naturally, but we're taught to focus on our problems.
- We often feel entitled to having a good life, as if the world owes us.
- True gratitude means being grateful for everything we're given—even life itself.

*Not being grateful implies that
I don't think much of myself.
Being ungrateful means others
won't think much of me either.*

How can you fix it?

You can cultivate gratitude and appreciation by:

- actively thanking others, nature and yourself for all the bounty in your life
- accepting compliments graciously and taking time to notice and compliment others
- allowing yourself to gratefully receive the love, support or input of others
- reminding yourself that gratitude magnetizes good things to you
- going out of your way to give to others, for the sheer joy and pleasure of giving
- taking every opportunity to acknowledge and appreciate those around you
- creating simple daily rituals that remind you to focus on being grateful.

*The more grateful you are, the more grateful others are
to have you around, and the more grateful you feel,
the more generous you want to be.*

G gratitude & generosity

generosity

*the quality of being kind or magnanimous; readiness or liberality in giving [**of yourself, your time, your money, your love**]; freedom from meanness or smallness of mind/character [**freely being my authentic, loving, generous self**]*

Why is it important?

- Generosity indicates a healthy trust in self and in the universe to provide.
- Being generous affirms that we have plenty and that more is always coming to us.
- It keeps us open, connected to others and mindful of how interdependent we all are.
- Being generous inspires others to do the same and makes us all feel good.
- Generosity is more about wanting to pay it forward than wanting it to be paid back.
- Giving generously to someone in need can make a huge difference in their life.
- Being generous with praise, credit and support boosts confidence and self-esteem.
- Giving generously to others makes us feel good (it's not just about giving to them).

Being generous towards others benefits you as much as them.

What's the problem?

- If we don't have much money, we may want to hold on to what we've got.

- We don't realize that giving to others also benefits us emotionally.

- Being generous can sometimes mean giving more than feels comfortable.

- Generosity takes practice; it may not be comfortable, at first.

- We need to also be comfortable with receiving–letting things in as well as out.

- We often focus on accumulating material things rather than giving of ourselves.

- We don't realize that our small efforts or donations can make a difference.

- It takes courage to reach out to someone in need; we're afraid of getting involved.

May the G-force be with you!

How can you fix it?

You can become more generous by:

- giving something small to someone every day, even if it's just a smile

- giving unconditionally, for the joy of it, without expecting anything in return

- simplifying your life so you're happy with less and have more to give

- being warm and generous with your praise, love and friendship

- opening your heart to others and feeling good about giving

- allowing others to give to you, too, because you know how good it feels to give

- reminding yourself that we're all connected; giving to others means giving to self

- supporting something you believe in, with values and a philosophy you share

- finding greater purpose and fulfillment by giving intentionally and spontaneously.

Being generous makes you realize
how much you have to give.

H honesty & happiness

honesty

integrity, trustworthiness, openness [**with my feelings and values**]; *truthfulness, sincerity or frankness* [**about my motives and actions**]; *freedom from deceit, fraud or manipulation*

Why is it important?

- Honesty builds trust; without it, people may not trust or like us.
- Honesty is vital for healthy relationships–and relationships are everything!
- Being honest means others can depend on us to tell the truth and do the right thing.
- Not being honest in your interactions or business dealings always backfires.
- Honesty cultivates greater openness and friendship.
- Emotional honesty is the most important quality in any intimate relationship.
- When we do the right thing, even if it seems daunting, there's always some reward.
- Being honest enhances our self-esteem and makes us feel good about ourselves.
- Honesty means not just being true to others but also being true to ourselves.

*Honesty means not having to remember
what you said or why you said it.*

What's the problem?

- We've been taught to use lies and manipulation as a way to get what we want.
- We're often afraid to tell the truth in case we get into trouble.
- We don't always have the courage to admit when we've done something wrong.
- If we feel unworthy or ashamed, we may want to hide things from others.
- Our fear of rejection often causes us to avoid telling the whole truth.
- If we're in any kind of abusive or critical relationship, honesty may not feel safe.
- We often blame others when something goes wrong, avoiding responsibility.
- We may argue that we're protecting someone's feelings by not being really honest.

Only by being honest with yourself
can you know who you are
and then be honest with others.

How can you fix it?

You can practise/strive for greater honesty by:

- digging deep to get to the truth inside yourself
- not settling for quick/bland answers but really considering your words before you speak
- bearing in mind that honesty is an expression of love and respect for self and others
- staying connected to and processing your feelings so you know what's true for you
- taking your time when making decisions or giving feedback/opinions to others
- remembering that honesty is a measure of your integrity, which means honouring you
- being honest and open in your relationships, without being critical or judgemental
- being honest with the small stuff–such as returning something someone lost
- remembering that honesty takes courage and has a powerful positive impact.

Honestly sharing yourself with others
makes you happy to be you.

H honesty & happiness

happiness

*a state of well-being and contentment; a feeling of deep satisfaction and pleasure [**rocket fuel for humans**]*

Why is it important?

- Experiencing happiness is what makes us feel good and life worthwhile.
- We may strive for wealth, prominence or acclaim but we're all seeking happiness.
- The more happiness we experience, the better people we become.
- When we're happy, we focus on the good things, which brings us more of them.
- Our happiness quotient is a measure of how fully and lovingly we're living life.
- Experiencing happiness makes us more compassionate, generous and understanding.
- Happiness enhances our health, relationships, creativity and optimism.
- Without happiness, we can become negative, cynical, argumentative or violent.
- Focusing on happiness rather than on success enables us to achieve more.

*Happiness is a warm fuzzy feeling
with a big dose of joyful excitement.*

What's the problem?

- We're often so focused on success that we forget the importance of being happy.
- We may not realize that happiness is a powerful magnetic force.
- Money, possessions and achievements are usually seen as a sign of success.
- Our culture of consumerism distracts us from peace and contentment.
- We are taught to use our logical minds more than our hearts.
- Negativity can be contagious, but then so can happiness...

The more I accept myself as I am,
the happier I feel.

How can you fix it?

You can generate more happiness by:

- expressing yourself from the heart about what matters to you
- reaching out to others and making a heartfelt connection
- focusing on all the blessings in your life and being grateful for them
- complimenting others and enjoying their pleasure at being appreciated
- focusing more on feelings than on circumstances
- laughing more and making time for fun and playfulness
- going out of your way to give to others and to bring little gifts to your friends
- sharing something meaningful with people you meet, not just polite platitudes
- sitting in nature/by the ocean and absorbing its wonderful, uplifting energy
- spending time with positive people and sharing your positive thoughts.

Happiness is a choice,
agreed to by your heart,
your mind and your body.

integration

the act of combining/adding parts to make a unified whole; absorbing or processing the experiences of life; the organization of personality traits/tendencies into a harmonious whole

Why is it important?

- We need downtime in order to integrate our experiences and know what we feel.
- Without healthy integration, we may not know what we want or make wise choices.
- We need integration for creative thinking and to process our intuitive responses.
- Healthy integration allows our body and mind to make sense of things.
- Without integration, we may stay stuck in overwhelm, negative cycles and reactivity.
- With it, we can process, heal, catch up with, and be present to, what's going on.
- It allows for a deeper connection with self and with one's inner guidance/inspiration.
- With integration, we hit the 'pause' button, allowing life to happen with more ease.

*Only by fully integrating our feelings
can we truly know what we want.*

What's the problem?

- Our high-speed living means we rarely fully process/integrate our experiences.
- We are constantly being stimulated by outside distractions.
- We can get stuck in negative cycles, not realizing that we need time out.
- We need to 'de-frag' our mental computer to make room for more things to come in.
- The more things we are juggling at once, the more we need to integrate them.
- In our modern Western society, the emphasis is on doing rather than being.
- We are rarely taught the art of being present and processing things in the moment.

The more we process our experiences,
the more fulfillment we get from them.

How can you fix it?

You can practise healthier integration by:

- taking time out every day to integrate everything that has happened to you
- allowing yourself to sit quietly so your body and mind can process things and relax
- connecting with your deeper, inner guidance so your decisions/choices become clear
- choosing not to chase things, since it usually pushes them away
- focusing on being grounded and aware, so you get out of your own way
- meditating whenever you feel overwhelmed or stressed
- always processing your feelings so that you know what's driving you/your choices
- expressing any confusion to others so you get clarity about what you really want
- reminding yourself that the answers are inside; you just need to process what you feel.

True enlightenment comes from integrating all the
many parts of you; only then can you experience
true intimacy with another.

intimacy

close or warm friendship or understanding; personal relationship
[a deep and meaningful connection with another]; sexual relations

Why is it important?

- Intimacy is more than sexual closeness; it's authenticity coupled with vulnerability.
- It is the naked exposure and/or sharing of our deepest feelings.
- It's about sharing our doubts, fears, grief, shame, affection, love, passion and spirit.
- It's self-expression without façade, control, contrivance, manipulation or inhibition.
- Nothing creates greater intimacy than the sharing of our deepest wounds.
- It is about openly sharing our wobbles and weaknesses as well as our strengths.
- Intimacy means uniting with another–through our words, attention, hearts, etc.
- True and meaningful sexual intimacy comes from honest emotional sharing.
- Without true intimacy, life can seem shallow, meaningless and lonely.

When we allow ourselves
to be vulnerable and authentic,
we can finally sink into intimacy.

What's the problem?

- Raw honesty does not come easily to most people.

- We've been taught to hide certain parts of ourselves, in order to be socially acceptable.

- We often believe that it's not safe to be emotionally vulnerable, as others can hurt us.

- If we're afraid of being hurt, we devise strategies for avoiding or deflecting closeness.

- We often learn to use humour, sarcasm and flippancy to keep others at a distance.

- An active mind and body cancel out the possibility of a still heart and spirit.

- We may use the busyness of our lives as a distraction from going deeper with others.

Hiding our wounds just keeps us wounded;
openly, lovingly sharing them
allows them to finally dissolve.

How can you fix it?

You can practise and generate greater intimacy by:

- being open and honest from the very core of your being

- refusing to use distancing tactics such as humour or criticism to keep people at bay

- creating opportunities for physical, emotional and spiritual closeness

- allowing your innate femininity or masculinity to blossom

- allowing your deepest feelings to surface, no matter how scary it may be to share them

- surrendering to the love and passion between you and your partner

- clearing obstacles to closeness (distance, other commitments, fears, doubts)

- dropping your façades or any attempts to appear to be other than what/who you are

- learning to be comfortable with joy and passion, as well as grief

- loving yourself enough to allow someone you love to love you.

Only when you find and love all the aspects of you
can you lose all inhibitions with another.

J

judgement
& justice

judgement

*the ability to judge [**character, values and friendships**] or make sound decisions; form an opinion objectively and wisely [**ideally prompting positive, empowered action**]; the evaluation of evidence in the making of a decision*

Why is it important?

- We need good judgement to know what's best for us and to make wise decisions.
- Without it, we may choose unsuitable friendships or business partners.
- We need sound judgement in order to do well in our career or relationships.
- Good judgement requires awareness, discernment and observation.
- It's our own version of wisdom, based on learning, listening, watching and feeling.
- When we exercise good judgement, we gain the respect and admiration of others.
- Leaders, teachers or people of influence need to make well-informed judgements.
- Good judgement is also needed in understanding and relating to others.

The judgements we make of others
often say more about us than them.

What's the problem?

- Our own feelings and negative experiences often cloud our judgement.
- Need, fear and unfounded beliefs can distort our judgement.
- Sometimes, the more advice we get, the more confused we become.
- We may get swayed by hype or smooth talking.
- If our values get compromised, so will our judgement.
- Stress or pressure can affect our judgement.
- Our judgement can be distorted by being with negative people.

Learning how to think versus what to think is one of the most powerful life skills we can develop.

How can you fix it?

You can enhance your ability to make sound judgements by:

- becoming more aware of what you feel when you're talking to people
- noticing any unease, stress or tension that you feel in certain situations
- watching body language and the confidence of others
- being an attentive listener so that you can fully process what you're hearing
- picking up on any sub-text that may lie beneath someone's words
- keeping an open mind when exploring new situations or relationships
- being direct and speaking the truth, which encourages others to do the same
- noticing how others handle your directness, and what that tells you about them.

Only when you clean the lens through which you judge, can you do everyone justice.

J

judgement
& justice

justice

the principle of moral rightness; fair, equitable treatment/ judgement/reward, in accordance with honour, standards or law [and what is morally right]; right action [based on personal values and integrity]

Why is it important?

- A healthy sense of justice within ourselves cultivates fairness and integrity.
- Doing ourselves justice means validating and making full use of our abilities.
- A just and ethical code of conduct helps keep us all respectful of each other.
- Our conscience (or personal sense of justice) tells us what feels morally right/wrong.
- When society fosters fairness, we are more likely to be fair to others.
- Doing what's morally right and being fair to others usually feels good.
- Justice is its own reward, but there are often tangible rewards, too.

True justice begins in our heart and is translated by our conscience.

What's the problem?

- We're not always taught to make a clear distinction between right and wrong.
- Doing ourselves justice requires healthy self-worth, which many of us lack.
- Always doing what's morally right requires strength of character and trust in self.
- True justice means taking full responsibility for who we are and what we do.
- We're taught that life's not fair, so we're not surprised when it isn't.
- Doing the right thing sometimes requires more effort than allowing things to be wrong.

Most of us are too busy trying to get things right to care about justice for others.

How can you fix it?

You can cultivate a greater sense of justice in your life by:

- being guided by your conscience in everything you do
- living by your values rather than merely articulating them
- sticking to the truth, no matter how scary that might feel
- allowing yourself to feel compassion for others, even if you cannot fix their lives
- keeping yourself informed about what's happening in your community
- voting for what's right and petitioning against what's wrong
- not purchasing products/commodities that have a negative impact on others
- participating in community events that improve the lives of the vulnerable
- buying from Fair Trade retailers/wholesalers as much as you can
- becoming more aware of how your actions and consumer choices affect others.

Justice combined with wisdom and compassion produces the best possible outcomes for all.

K

kindness & keenness

kindness

*caring in action [**acting from the heart**]; the practice or quality of being kind [**towards self and others**]; a considerate or helpful act [**with no expectations or conditions**]*

Why is it important?

- Kindness is more than just being nice; it's humanity with heartfelt action.
- We all need kindness to brighten our lives and help us weather the tough bits.
- Kindness is the antidote to cruelty, bullying, ignorance and abuse.
- It's about taking action to help others, not just feeling sympathy for them.
- We all need loving kindness (but if we have to ask for it, it doesn't feel right).
- Kindness is what makes us human, connecting us all through the heart.
- It's contagious and makes us all feel good.
- It's not based on merit; it's unconditional giving, with compassion and respect.

No matter how small our acts of kindness may seem, they will always have an impact somewhere —even if it's just inside us.

What's the problem?

- Words are cheap and easy, but acts of kindness require time and energy.
- We've become hardened by seeing too much hardship, tragedy and loss in the media.
- Many of us are so busy trying to make our lives work that we forget to give.
- We may be afraid that people will abuse our kindness or not appreciate it.
- We don't realize that kindness is as much about giving to ourselves as to others.
- We may feel as if we can't really help others (such as the homeless) in meaningful ways.
- If we think we can't help, we may choose not to get involved, and do nothing.

If we hold back kindness,
we're putting our hearts on hold.

How can you fix it?

You can become a kinder person by:

- stopping to talk to the homeless or helping children/the elderly in your community
- making eye contact with others, and connecting with compassion and caring
- being more aware of those around you and reaching out to them
- reminding yourself that kindness softens your heart and keeps you open/receptive
- expressing your feelings and gratitude for those close to you
- appreciating your body and every breath you take, so you value the life in others
- giving of your time and energy, even if it doesn't feel significant
- getting involved in community activities or soup kitchens to help others
- donating to worthy causes and giving what you can to those on the street
- becoming a Big Brother/Sister or mentor to young people in your community.

The more you cultivate kindness in your life,
the more keenly you experience your own value.

K

kindness
& keenness

keenness

*exceptional discernment, judgement or perception [**extreme sensitivity or responsiveness**]; great mental penetration or acumen; strong feeling or desire/enthusiasm [**very much wanting something to happen**]*

Why is it important?

- Being keen shows interest, enthusiasm and energy for something or someone.
- We all need energy and enthusiasm to accomplish our goals.
- When we're keen, we get things done; we get others fired up, too.
- Being keen helps us stay motivated, vibrant and on track, with a sense of purpose.
- Sharing our enthusiasm with others usually helps to sharpen their interest.
- Having a keenness of perception/judgement serves us well in decision-making.
- A strong desire for something to happen pushes us to overcome any obstacles.
- Having a keen mind means being alert to what's going on/what others are saying.
- Discernment can make the difference between success and failure.

Taking a keen interest in something, no matter how banal, gives it meaning and magnetism.

What's the problem?

- With the stresses of modern living, many of us have given up on our dreams.

- If we are burnt out from work/family/relationships, we may have lost our zest for life.

- With so many online distractions and so much multi-tasking, we can lose our edge.

- If we're overwhelmed with too many demands, we may flat-line or go numb.

- If we don't stay active and fit, our minds tend to switch off and become lethargic

- With the media so full of sensationalism, it's easy to become jaded and cynical.

Staying responsive to life
keeps life responding to you.

How can you fix it?

You can develop greater keenness by:

- mindfully experiencing the world through all of your senses

- slowing down so that you can really feel and enjoy the good things in life

- staying alert to signs/opportunities, to open doors you might not have noticed

- not giving energy to things in which you don't feel keenly interested

- expressing enthusiasm for new ideas, other people's projects, and everyone's dreams

- enthusiastically feeling, feeding and envisioning your success/ideal outcome

- allowing time for quiet reflection so you stay focused on your deeper feelings

- exercising and eating well so that you keep up your energy, verve and vitality

- learning new things and keeping your mind engaged, clear and sharp.

How keen you are about something is
a measure of your faith in yourself.

L love & laughter

love

*an intense feeling of deep affection [**warm and tender feelings towards another**]; a strong attraction and personal attachment; human kindness, caring, compassion and acceptance*

Why is it important?

- Love keeps us all connected and aspiring towards higher things.
- It motivates us to be our best, as we all want to be loved and accepted by others.
- It facilitates our interpersonal relationships and keeps the species going.
- Experiencing true love in our lives fills us with optimism, joy and vitality.
- Love is about giving, sharing, supporting, forgiving, uplifting and caring for others.
- Having love in our lives makes us happier and healthier. We need it.
- Love engenders feelings that foster a healthier, more compassionate world.
- Healthy self-love is essential for healthy relationships.

Love is the universal glue that keeps us all connected.

What's the problem?

- Love often gets confused with need, leading to co-dependent relationships.
- Unconditional love is exceedingly rare, and most people lack self-love/acceptance.
- If we cannot love, accept or be ourselves, our relationships become dysfunctional.
- If we grow up with abuse/disrespect/neglect, it can get handed down to our children.
- We're taught that self-love is selfish (yet it's how we learn to love others).
- If we're too eager to be loved/accepted by others, we make unhealthy compromises.
- Need-based, loveless relationships create more problems than they solve.

If we love to be needed,
we're nowhere near love at all.

How can you fix it?

You can bring more love into your heart and your life by:

- focusing on cultivating love inside yourself, versus seeking it outside of you
- practising love/acceptance for self/others, so you're a magnet for more of the same
- staying connected to your feelings so that you can really connect with others
- taking care of you by eating well, exercising, resting and being with good friends
- not making compromises that don't feel right (as they always backfire)
- sharing laughter, smiles, warmth and affection with everyone in your life
- looking for ways to express love, kindness and understanding to those close to you
- doing what you love so you can love what you do—and be happy, healthy and fulfilled.

Love is the spark that ignites your creativity, passion
and zest for life, bringing lightness and laughter.

L

laughter

the experience/manifestation of mirth, amusement, joy or delight **[the bubbling up of the happiness we feel inside]**; *an expression of exultant well-being* **[and our sense of humour]**

Why is it important?

- Laughter lightens our spirit and lights up our face.
- It decreases stress and tension while enhancing our mood.
- Laughter is infectious and magnetic, drawing others to us and making them smile.
- Humour and laughter can defuse conflict/tension/resentment, and enhance teamwork.
- Laughter energizes the whole body and boosts the immune system.
- It revitalizes the body's organs, releases endorphins and enhances circulation.
- Laughter increases happiness, intimacy and feelings of connectedness.
- It relaxes the muscles and decreases physical and emotional pain.
- Laughter reduces our problems and lengthens our lives.

Laughing is like suddenly remembering that life is meant to be fun.

What's the problem?

- If we get stressed or overworked, we often take ourselves too seriously.
- If life is a struggle, we may not think there's anything to laugh about.
- The more we focus on our problems, the less we feel like laughing.
- We don't realize that laughter and humour can lift us out of a funk.
- We're often unaware of the powerful healing force of laughter.
- If we're tense or stressed, laughter is the last thing we think of yet what we most need.
- Laughter may seem too frivolous for the workplace (yet it fosters collaboration).

If we can't laugh at ourselves,
someone else will.

How can you fix it?

You can bring more laughter into your life by:

- watching funny movies/videos and letting yourself have fun
- always looking for the humour in any tense or stressful situation
- seeing the humour in the many ironies of life
- sharing laughter with friends–and everyone you meet
- remembering that laughter lightens the load and stimulates creativity
- enhancing learning through laughter–for you and for those you teach/support
- using humour in talks/workshops/interactions to instil confidence and trust
- going out of your way to have fun and keep your body enlivened with laughter
- researching and sharing some really good jokes
- laughing alone every day because it heals you, lifts you and makes you feel good.

Laughter is the cheapest universal way
to bring people together.

M mastery & manifestation

mastery

*superior command of something [**and of self/life's principles**]; victory; expert skill, knowledge or technique [**in being powerfully, creatively, expressively, authentically human**]*

Why is it important?

- Self-mastery means being in charge of our body, our mind and our emotions.
- Changing our minds about who we are/what we can do changes everything.
- When we understand universal principles, we can apply them, to positive effect.
- We can live powerfully, positively and purposefully when we master our minds.
- Mastery of anything (including self) requires complete conviction in ourselves.
- Mastering ourselves and becoming empowered is our biggest challenge in life.
- There is nothing more rewarding than consciously creating the life we want.

If we're not in charge of our own emotions, someone else is.

What's the problem?

- We're taught to react to our world rather than proactively shaping it.
- We spend most of our time and energy reacting to life as it 'happens'.
- We're not taught that our circumstances reflect what's going on in our minds.
- Life is colourful, demanding and dramatic, distracting us from what's going on inside.
- Because other people can cause us to react emotionally, we think they're the problem.
- If we don't realize we're powerful, we'll tend to become victims and blame others.
- We're rarely taught to take full responsibility for ourselves, or how to do that.
- The way we are programmed, early in life, determines the course of our lives.

*Our programming is the very thing that
gets in the way of us realizing that it's the very thing
that's getting in our way.*

How can you fix it?

You can cultivate greater self-mastery by:

- becoming more aware of when you're emotionally triggered, and why
- gaining a deeper understanding of how your subconscious mind works
- filling in your missing pieces so you attract what's been missing in your life
- exploring the idea that your subconscious programming is running the show
- identifying the negative beliefs that hinder your performance and success
- taking full responsibility for your choices, emotions and reactions.
- seeing any negative circumstances as clues to what's missing inside you
- realizing that mastering your mind is the key to mastering your life.

*When positively programmed,
your subconscious becomes your greatest ally
in manifesting what you want.*

M mastery & manifestation

manifestation

*the act or process of manifesting/making real; a perceptible, outward or visible expression [**of the self**]; a demonstration of power and purpose [**in making relationships, career, finances and life work beautifully**]*

Why is it important?

- Manifesting what we want in life makes it rewarding and worthwhile.
- When we can manifest positive outcomes, we can fulfil much more of our potential.
- Being able to manifest what we want means we're empowered and on track with self.
- Having a sense of control over our destiny gives us a sense of purpose.
- We're more inspired, positive and creative when we can manifest positive outcomes.
- Proactively manifesting is like magic—and it's fun!

We can create magic in our lives
when we operate from the inside out.

What's the problem?

- We rarely understand the true drivers of our life's circumstances.
- We're always manifesting, even if we don't realize it–though not always positively.
- If we're negatively programmed, we'll manifest more of what we don't want.
- We don't realize that we manifest a reflection of what's going on inside.
- Unless we change them, our negative beliefs generate negative circumstances.
- We're rarely taught the principles of powerfully manifesting what we want.
- We don't understand what our circumstances represent.
- Circumstances reflect the negative programming in us that's asking to be addressed.

We're taught to defer to religions, politics and authority rather than being in charge of ourselves.

How can you fix it?

You can become more 'manifestatious' by:

- identifying negative beliefs that don't support you in being powerful
- countering all thoughts that lead you to doubt yourself or hold back
- behaving and speaking as if you're confident and more than good enough
- eliminating all words, actions and compromises that don't feel good
- expressing your opinions, feelings and creativity in all that you do
- breathing deeply and exercising your abdominal area, which helps you manifest
- making sure that your words and actions are in alignment with your values
- recognizing that circumstances are clues about what needs to change inside
- giving yourself permission to be honest, open and authentic with others.

Every circumstance in your life is perfectly aligned with your greater purpose: to be fully, powerfully you.

N

nourishment & nurturing

nourishment

sustenance necessary for life, growth, health and well-being [at the physical, emotional, mental and spiritual levels]

Why is it important?

- We all need physical, emotional and spiritual nourishment to be balanced and well.
- Without healthy nourishment, we fail to thrive or maybe even survive.
- Nourishment with love, acceptance, respect and trust breeds healthy, loving humans.
- Emotional malnourishment leads to all kinds of physical symptoms and disease.
- We need healthy emotional nourishment in order to have healthy relationships.
- If we nourish ourselves spiritually, we feel better emotionally and physically.
- When we are nourished on all levels, we feel balanced, healthy, vital and fulfilled.

With a happy heart, a healthy bod and a carefree spirit, we can thrive and love life.

What's the problem?

- We are rarely taught the principles of healthy eating, let alone emotional expression.
- As children, we rarely learn how to process our emotions, so we suppress them.
- If we experience fear or insecurity, growing up, we hold on to those fears as adults.
- Our fast-paced living is not conducive to emotional healing or quiet contemplation.
- If we're emotionally/spiritually disconnected, we may lack compassion or feeling.
- If we are not nourished emotionally, we feel a gnawing hunger for love and comfort.
- Without healthy nourishment, we may resort to comfort foods and negative behaviours.

If we're starved of love,
we can be all-consuming in relationships.

How can you fix it?

You can nourish yourself emotionally, physically and spiritually by:

- meditating, exercising, doing breathwork/yoga and being in nature
- eating wholesome, healthy foods so that your body/mind is balanced and clear
- spending time with a loving friend/partner who supports you emotionally/physically
- taking care of your own needs, in healthy ways, so you're not needy with others
- getting lots of sunlight on your skin, to keep your mood buoyant
- expressing gratitude for all the things that do nourish you
- finding healthy ways to vent any pent-up/suppressed emotions
- listening to soothing or uplifting music to feed your soul.

Feed your body, mind and spirit with top-notch fuel,
and you'll motor through life
like a finely-tuned Porsche.

N

nurturing

encouragement, caring, love or support; the cultivation and fostering of healthy growth and development [done with gentleness and care]

Why is it important?

- Loving care and tenderness are vital for intimacy and emotional fulfillment.
- Being cared for with love and gentleness makes us more loving and giving.
- When we're nurtured, we feel strong, self-assured and happy in ourselves.
- Nurturing ourselves means cultivating softness as well as kindness to self.
- It means embracing our imperfections and accepting ourselves as we are.
- Nurturing our spirituality means listening to our intuition versus our logic.
- Tenderness opens the door to honest, intimate, open communication and trust.

*Nurturing ourselves is like having
our own private little sanctuary.*

What's the problem?

- Men, particularly, are often taught that tenderness is for sissies.
- Without nurturing, we can become distant, depressed or emotionally buffered.
- As consumers, we tend to focus more on what we have than on what we feel.
- Having time to truly care for–and give to–others has become a rarity.
- We often learn to keep our hearts closed to protect ourselves from being hurt.
- We don't realize that nurturing others is also a way of nurturing ourselves.
- The stress of modern living tends to disconnect us from our body's needs.

If we're too tough to be tender,
love and intimacy will have a hard time getting in.

How can you fix it?

You can bring more nurturing into your life by:

- allowing yourself to be loved, touched, held and appreciated by your partner
- taking time to be tender–with your words, actions and gestures
- responding with gentleness when someone is feeling hurt or depressed
- understanding that anger and resentment often hide pain and sadness
- remembering to be just as gentle with yourself as you are with those you love
- acknowledging yourself whenever you do something loving/healthy for you
- reaching out to others who may seem closed off, sad or remote
- pampering yourself with hot baths, music, essential oils if you feel overwhelmed.

Tender words and nurturing touch can
open hearts and heal the deepest wounds.

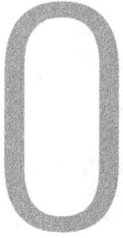

O optimism & originality

optimism

*hopefulness/confidence about the future or the success of something [**including self**]; focusing on positive aspects; expecting favourable outcomes; the belief that all is as it should be*

Why is it important?

- A positive outlook strengthens our immune system, reducing stress and ill-health.
- Optimism enables us to turn challenges into opportunities (rather than crises).
- If we always look for the 'blessing in disguise', we almost always find it.
- Optimists tend to believe that their positive actions result in positive outcomes.
- Being optimistic transmits positive energy, generating creativity and ideas.
- It's based on a belief that you can make things happen and have what you want.
- Optimism inspires and motivates, pushing us and others to take positive action.
- Anticipating positive things promotes a constructive, can-do attitude.
- Being optimistic makes you braver, happier, more confident and nicer to be with.

Optimists have a lot more fun,
and a lot more to look forward to.

What's the problem?

- Thinking positively is a popular concept, but it's not enough on its own.
- Optimism must be combined with positive action for magic to happen.
- Our positivity can easily be cancelled out by negative self-talk/beliefs.
- We may get sucked into dramas, conflicts or other unhealthy dynamics.
- If we believe that life just happens, we may live like victims of our circumstances.
- Without healthy optimism, we may find it hard to recover from setbacks or heartache.
- Thinking negatively about work, relationships or life reduces our chances of success.

If we're not positive about life,
life won't be positive about us.

How can you fix it?

You can generate more optimism in your life by:

- spending time with positive, optimistic people
- savouring and celebrating every positive thing that happens in your life
- trying new things so you can get excited about new possibilities
- remembering that, whatever happens, it's for a good reason—and you can find it!
- choosing to stay positive, regardless of the economy, weather, problems, etc
- sharing positive thoughts and outlooks with others so that it lifts them and you
- feeding your positive ideas and expectations by taking positive action
- knowing that you decide who you are and what you can be—and then being it
- fostering positivity, knowing that it breeds community, leadership and big ideas.

Optimism promotes openness,
which promotes opportunity,
which promotes originality...
which promotes more optimism.

O

optimism
& originality

originality

*the ability to think independently or creatively; the quality of being new or inventive [**or uniquely you**]*

Why is it important?

- We've all got something that no one else has, which makes life interesting.
- Our voice, creativity, humour, taste, opinions and style make us unique.
- Thinking creatively helps solve problems and leads to new discoveries.
- When we think independently or creatively, we find better ways of doing things.
- Our creativity feeds us–through music, art, architecture, song, poetry, writing.
- Our individual creativity contributes to the well-being and pleasure of all.
- Originality can put a new spin on things, helping us to see things in a new light.
- It can make learning fun, and it keeps us evolving as a species.

*Our originality lies in our imagination,
which is as vast and fertile as we allow it to be.*

What's the problem?

- Our creativity is often pushed aside in favour of more 'practical' things.
- Creativity is rarely valued as the precious, life-enhancing commodity that it is.
- Being creative/original means stepping out of the crowd, which many fear doing.
- Originality involves risk; your ideas may be ridiculed or invalidated.
- People tend to be critical of others, especially those who do outrageous things.
- Creativity is often seen as something frivolous, to be done during leisure time only.

Great ideas are rarely created by committee.

How can you fix it?

You can foster greater originality by:

- making time to sit quietly, muse, play, explore and have fun with others
- being okay with uncertainty, since originality involves new inspiration/ideas
- doing something creative (acting/art/writing/design/doodling) at least once a week
- engaging in creative activities without no fixed outcome in mind
- daring to speak out, stand out, be different and not blend in with the crowd
- enlivening your home/office with colours, textures and your own creative flair
- giving yourself creative challenges–such as inventing new words or definitions
- meditating and opening up to universal inspiration and thoughts
- changing your routine (and your perspective) in three key ways every day
- playing Tiddlywinks, blowing bubbles... to bring out your playful self.

Forget about using your logical brain;
have fun coaxing out the creative genius hiding inside.

P   passion
      & purpose

passion

*a powerful or compelling emotion/feeling [**motivating us to act or to express what feels important**]; boundless enthusiasm [**for something**]; strong amorous feeling or desire*

Why is it important?

- Pursuing our passions brings us happiness and fulfillment.
- Having a passion in life gives us something to strive for and work towards.
- Being passionate about something boosts our confidence and, often, our expertise.
- Pursuing our passions keeps us growing and reaching for our dreams.
- Living a passionate life usually means we're in touch with what matters to us.
- We tend to become very focused and 'on purpose' when pursuing our passions.
- What we're passionate about is often unique to us–something we can excel at.
- Living passionately boosts our energy, love life, health and joie de vivre.

Living our passion is contagious,
inspiring others to do the same.

What's the problem?

- We often opt for 'safety' rather than pursuing a passion.
- We may not know what our passion is, or how to find it.
- Without passion, we can be listless and empty, with no drive/sense of purpose.
- In choosing a career, we're often pushed into something 'sensible' vs exciting.
- We may lack passion (for life/our partner) if we've had a troubled childhood.
- Finding our passion may be hard if our creativity has been suppressed.
- Our passion can die if we stay stuck in an unfulfilling job or relationship.

If we're more concerned about our pension than our passion, we'll end up having more regrets than benefits.

How can you fix it?

You can get in touch with your passion by:

- being honest with yourself about what you dislike about your life–and why
- exploring what you enjoy doing and having fun doing it
- learning a new hobby or skill in some area that interests you
- changing your routine so your mind stays fresh, alert and expectant
- noticing what kinds of things you like to read, do, talk about or research
- brainstorming with others about your ideas and what inspires you
- trying something new and taking yourself out of your comfort zone
- volunteering so that you can try out some different skills/activities
- travelling to new places/cultures to help you get inspired.

When you're purposeful about your passion, you'll end up being passionate about your purpose.

P passion & purpose

purpose

*a strong resolve or determination; the reason for which something is done/created [**the reason for one's existence**]; an aim or intention*

Why is it important?

- Having a sense of purpose in life gives us direction and meaning.
- Defining our purpose takes us on a path towards self-betterment and fulfillment.
- When we have a strong sense of purpose, we are less easily swayed/defined by others.
- We feel empowered, focused and present when we have a purpose to our lives.
- Living life on purpose means living in accordance with our values and beliefs.
- Living purposefully usually means being committed to being the best that we can be.
- Fulfilling our purpose often involves collaborating with others, bringing rewards for all.
- When we have a meaningful purpose, we feel more at peace with ourselves.

Our purpose is to be truly, fully, powerfully ourselves, whatever that looks like.

What's the problem?

- We're often so caught up in what others tell us to do that we cannot find our purpose.
- Finding our own purpose takes time and effort–plus a determination to succeed.
- We may get thrown off track by religious dogma and other belief systems.
- Meeting others' needs may feel like our true purpose... but it rarely is.
- We may feel that making a lot of money is our purpose... but that's rarely it, either.
- We're often too stressed and distracted to be able to get in touch with our purpose.
- Feeling unmotivated can get us stuck in a cycle of not wanting to explore things.
- If we have too many competing priorities, it's hard to get clear about our true purpose.

If we keep doing what others say we should do,
we'll end up living for them instead of for us.

How can you fix it?

You can get more in touch/on track with your purpose by:

- checking that you're living in alignment with your values and beliefs
- being aware of how you feel about particular people, projects or passions in your life
- regularly re-assessing your friendships, activities, relationships and work
- staying present and living in the moment as much as possible
- being aware of when you lack momentum–and exploring why
- meditating/taking time out to gain more clarity about what you feel called to do
- not getting distracted by things that do not feed, inspire or uplift you
- exploring and noticing what brings you peace of mind–and body.

When you live life on purpose,
you realize that nothing is an accident.

Q quietude & quintessence

quietude

a state of stillness, calmness or tranquillity in a person or place; a Buddha-like composure; inner peace

Why is it important?

- Sitting in stillness enables us to process emotions, thoughts and intuitive insights.
- We need peace and tranquillity in order to recharge our batteries.
- Cultivating stillness through meditation boosts our health and immune systems.
- By stilling our minds, we reduce our stress levels and promote self-awareness.
- When we sit in quiet reflection, many things become clear, without effort.
- Stillness and peace bring presence of mind and a healthy perspective.
- Meditation enables us to connect with our deeper self and sense of purpose.
- Only when we are peaceful and silent can we sense our spiritual connection.

*Being at peace means
allowing ourselves to come home to our hearts.*

What's the problem?

- We live in a fast-paced, noisy world where peace and tranquillity are rare.
- We are so intent on doing that we have trouble just being.
- Our bodies and minds are not designed for constant action and thinking.
- We are often so physically and mentally exhausted that peace seems impossible.
- Our bodies are so used to being driven by adrenaline that it's hard to switch off.
- If we are stressed/busy, we don't breathe properly, which creates agitation.
- A restless mind is easily distracted by what's going on outside, versus inside.
- We tend to think our way through problems rather than tapping into our inner wisdom.

Without stillness,
we are moving targets
that are hard for others to reach.

How can you fix it?

You can generate greater quietude in your life by:

- taking time out every day to sit quietly, alone, for 15–30 minutes
- focusing on your breath, especially when in meetings or stressful situations
- cutting out unnecessary activities, conversations and interactions
- allowing for silence, rather than always having the TV or radio on
- relaxing your body through gentle yoga or moving meditation
- avoiding stimulants such as sugar, coffee and caffeinated drinks
- practising mindfulness in your daily routine—while eating, exercising, etc
- defusing stress by working the body whenever the mind becomes too active
- talking less and listening more.

Only with presence of mind
can the mind present its true essence.

Q quietude & quintessence

quintessence

*the pure, highly concentrated essence of a thing [**or person**]; the purest or most perfect embodiment of something [**such as you**]*

Why is it important?

- There's nothing more important than being quintessentially yourself.
- Being purely you is the only way to attract the perfect match for that.
- Being you is what you're designed to be best at–for a reason.
- It enables you to get in touch with your gifts, talents and purpose in life.
- There is power and magic in you being uncompromisingly you.
- Expressing your essential nature, values and passion brings freedom and fulfillment.
- Embodying the purest expression of you means trusting and loving who you are.
- It's a lot more rewarding and a lot less work to be yourself than to be fake.
- It's also your roadmap to happiness.

Being essentially you is... well, essential.

What's the problem?

- We're often taught to be something that we're not, in the hope of acceptance.
- We may never have glimpsed our true essence, or know how to access it.
- If we're focused on getting others' love/approval, we lose touch with our true self.
- The expectations and demands of others often cause us to distort who we are.
- Who we've been programmed to be usually has little to do with who we really are.
- Staying true to ourselves is generally not encouraged by society.
- It means stepping away from the crowd and daring to stand out.
- More value and importance are placed on what we do than on who we are.

*Only when you show who you really are
can you grow into who you really are.*

How can you fix it?

You can embody more of your quintessential self by:

- exploring your essence: is it creativity, dynamism, contemplation, etc?
- identifying what supports it (quiet time, being in nature, music, conversation)
- striving to live and operate in accordance with your natural essence
- noticing when your words/actions are not in alignment with your nature
- meditating/reflecting on what kind of friends, foods, lifestyle and work nourish you
- processing your emotions daily so you stay clear about what you're really feeling
- exploring your deeper nature through art, writing or other forms of self-expression
- always affirming that being true to you is the key to your success and happiness.

*It's not being true to you that's hard;
it's trying to be someone that you're not.*

R

responsibility
& receiving

responsibility

*being accountable for something/someone within one's power [**such as you**]; the ability to respond; the ability/authority to act and make decisions independently [**about your own life**]*

Why is it important?

- Taking responsibility for our beliefs, words and actions empowers us.
- We're accountable for our behaviour, rather than blaming others.
- Responsibility means owning our successes as well as any failures.
- We gain respect and trust from others when we demonstrate healthy responsibility.
- When we take responsibility for our lives, we're not hapless victims of circumstance.
- We act more responsibly when we know that we're answerable for what we do or say.
- We also know that we're not responsible for the feelings/actions/reactions of others.
- Being responsible for self encourages us to take better care of ourselves and our world.

*Responsibility means
owning our greatness—and living it.*

What's the problem?

- We're rarely taught that we're responsible for creating our own circumstances.
- We're not taught how to use our personal power to create what we want.
- We're often afraid to take responsibility, for fear of getting into trouble.
- Because we're generally not empowered, we fear the power/authority of others.
- We're disempowered by negative programming via education, religion, etc.
- We lack faith in ourselves to take control of our lives and our relationships.
- We're rarely taught to live life based on solid, healthy values.
- If we lack moral/social responsibility, we usually live at the expense of others.

If you're not taking responsibility for your life, who is...?

How can you fix it?

You can generate greater responsibility by:

- taking charge of your own life and allowing others to take charge of theirs
- remembering that taking responsibility for someone else disempowers you both
- catching yourself if you find you're blaming others/life for your circumstances
- always owning your choices and decisions, as well as your feelings and reactions
- doing whatever's required to resolve any unhealthy behaviour, feelings, regrets, etc
- maintaining healthy boundaries so you don't take on other people's problems
- acting/speaking powerfully and honestly with everyone in your life
- living your life as if you're in charge of everything that happens (which you are).

When you love being powerfully in charge of you, you're open to receiving.

R responsibility & receiving

receiving

acquiring something given; welcoming or allowing in someone/something [such as love, recognition, money etc]; having something bestowed upon, delivered/brought to oneself

Why is it important?

- Giving and receiving are part of the natural flow of life, keeping us connected.
- Being open to receiving means we're open to life's natural flow of abundance.
- When we have healthy self-worth, we are open to receiving from others/the universe.
- Allowing ourselves to receive love/support from others demonstrates self-acceptance.
- It also nourishes us, enhancing our health and boosting our self-confidence.
- Receiving means allowing others to love us and to enjoy the gift of giving.
- Graciously accepting compliments is one simple way of receiving love/recognition.
- Saying YES to receiving means we are open to being supported by the universe.
- Allowing ourselves to receive opens the door to more love, abundance and ease.

When we allow others in,
we allow ourselves to come out.

What's the problem?

- We are often taught that it's selfish to take and far more noble to give to others.
- Early negative programming may leave us feeling undeserving and unable to receive.
- We then tend to focus on giving rather than receiving, which blocks our prosperity.
- If we 'give to get', hoping for something in return, our neediness pushes others away.
- We may readily reject compliments and support if we lack healthy self-worth.
- If we always focus on giving vs receiving, we can become exhausted and resentful.
- If we're overly independent/self-sufficient, it prevents others from loving/reaching us.
- If we have difficulty receiving love/affection, it usually means that our hearts are closed.

If we're not open to receiving,
the universe will stop making deliveries.

How can you fix it?

You can open up to receiving more love, ease, money, etc by:

- saying YES to being supported or helped by others
- graciously accepting compliments, rather than qualifying or rejecting them
- asking for help and support when you need or want it
- sharing your opinions and deeper feelings in genuine, heartfelt ways
- being open to intimacy and emotional honesty with loved ones
- consciously saying YES to opportunities, invitations or expressions of love
- saying NO to meeting others' needs at the expense of your own
- going out of your way to connect/communicate in meaningful, authentic ways
- sharing your thoughts, gifts, personality and presence with others.

When you demonstrate deservability,
you become a magnet for receiving
the good things in life.

S self-expression & sexuality

self-expression

expression of one's thoughts, feelings, ideas or creativity through speech, writing, behaviour, artistic activities, style or humour

Why is it important?

- Verbal/artistic/creative/physical self-expression is what makes us unique.
- Through healthy self-expression, we can experience the full spectrum of who we are.
- By expressing ourselves fully, we discover our strengths, weaknesses, passions etc.
- In expressing ourselves to others, we gain clarity about what we think/feel/believe.
- Self-expression helps us to connect with our deeper emotions and what we want in life.
- The more we express ourselves, the more we come to know and fulfill our potential.
- By honestly, authentically expressing who we are, we attract the ideal match for that.
- Expressing ourselves creatively and proactively generates positive, powerful results.

*Expressing ourselves fully is the best way
to find out who we really are.*

What's the problem?

- As children, we're often told that it's not okay to express our feelings or emotions.
- We're not taught that self-expression is our most powerful means of connecting.
- In our need for approval, we're often afraid to say what we really think or feel.
- We often don't feel safe expressing an opinion that others may not share.
- We may avoid expressing our unique style or flair so we don't stand out.
- Being creative can seem risky as it often involves doing something new and daring.

*If we suppress any part of ourselves,
we can only ever be partially fulfilled.*

How can you fix it?

You can enhance your self-expression by:

- daring to voice your opinion about things that matter to you
- speaking out if you have something to say or if it makes you feel good about you
- standing up for yourself if someone is being pushy, dismissive, critical or abusive
- saying NO to whatever doesn't work for you or feel right for you
- allowing yourself to laugh or express your real feelings, in the moment
- being creative in how you express yourself, rather than doing/saying what's expected
- expressing your sense of humour, even if no one else seems to get it
- dressing/presenting yourself in a way that reflects your personality/personal flair
- exploring your unique brand of creativity through art, music, acting, dance, singing, etc.

*One of the most powerful ways for you to express,
heal and share yourself is through the healthy,
joyous expression of your sexuality.*

S self-expression & sexuality

sexuality

*capacity for sexual feelings/experiences/responses [**the power of sexual magnetism and attraction**]; how we express and experience ourselves as sexual beings*

Why is it important?

- Sexuality can encompass romance, relationships, sensuality and companionship.
- It's also about how we relate to ourselves and others as male/female.
- Our sexuality is part of our personality and it affects our ability to love and be loved.
- If we're comfortable with our sexuality, we can fully embrace our femininity/masculinity.
- We can also enjoy a deep, intimate, uninhibited connection with our partner.
- Our sexual development has a huge impact on how we develop as individuals.
- Healthy sexuality fosters love, affection and sexual intimacy.
- This keeps us happy, healthy and energized, while enriching our lives.
- It generates health-boosting hormones such as estrogen (for women) and oxytocin.
- It boosts immunity & metabolism, slows aging, and reduces the risk of cancer/stroke.

Sexuality is like a cream bun in a world full of cabbage.

What's the problem?

- Many religions/cultures frown upon sexuality as immoral or shameful.

- We are often taught that it's not okay to love our bodies or to enjoy our sexuality.

- Many people feel too ashamed or afraid to explore or discuss their sexuality.

- Because it's usually not discussed as a healthy, normal aspect of life, it gets suppressed.

- If we suppress our sexuality, it affects our health, relationships and happiness.

- Our sexual expression can become distorted if it's not nurtured in a healthy way.

- If we cannot express our sexuality, we cannot fully express our power as individuals.

Our sexuality is something innate.
We cannot fake it, but we can allow it to flourish.

How you can fix it

You can generate healthier sexuality by:

- daring to discuss your values, attitudes and beliefs about your sexuality

- taking time to understand/express your sexual feelings, rather than suppressing them

- discussing any shame, guilt or discomfort—with a partner and/or a counsellor

- accepting and sharing affection, sensual touch and intimate thoughts with a loved one

- mindfully letting go of inhibitions so you can enjoy your sexuality and sensuality

- taking healthy control of your body, given your right to say yes/no to sex

- finding ways to express and connect more deeply with your own femininity/masculinity

- identifying any limiting/unhealthy beliefs imposed by your upbringing/religion/culture

- expressing your personal flair and sensuality in way you dress and present yourself

- choosing to be a powerful sexual being, guided by love and self-acceptance.

Worn with love and self-confidence,
your sexuality boosts your health,
creativity and personal magnetism.

trust
& transformation

trust

firm reliance on the integrity, ability, reliability or character of a person/thing; confident expectation of something; acceptance of what's presented, without evidence or investigation

Why is it important?

- Trust is the foundation of any business or healthy, loving, intimate relationship.
- We need a strong sense of trust in order to feel safe being ourselves with others.
- Knowing whether to trust someone or not is a key way of keeping ourselves safe.
- The more we trust our own intuition, the healthier our choices and decisions.
- Trusting ourselves puts us in touch with what's right and best for us.
- It also takes us where we're meant to go, bringing fulfillment/well-being/success.
- When we trust ourselves, we realize there are no negative consequences to being us.
- When we practise self-trust, we know that it's the most powerful, magnetic way to live.
- Only by trusting/acting on our intuition can we find our ideal path and partner in life.

Self-trust promotes emotional and physical safety; it's an internal shift, not an external mechanism.

What's the problem?

- Few of us are taught to trust ourselves or to act on our gut instincts/intuition.
- If self-trust is not cultivated in us as children, we will have trust issues in relationships.
- We will also tend to attract untrustworthy people and situations into our lives.
- Trusting can feel scary because it means being okay with uncertainty/not knowing.
- Building healthy self-trust is the key to attracting trustworthy people in all our dealings.
- We tend to focus on what's happening 'out there', yet we drive our own circumstances.
- Fear and paranoia cause us to attract situations that feed and confirm our fears.
- Feeding our fears and producing 'evidence' of their validity prevents us from trusting.

We can't trust others if we don't trust ourselves.

How can you fix it?

You can build greater self-trust by:

- noticing whenever your body or your mind feels uneasy about something
- not acting on/agreeing to something if you sense that it's not quite right
- saying NO to whatever doesn't feel right, especially if your trust is violated
- slowing down so you become aware of your gut feelings and what you feel drawn to do
- making choices/decisions based on what feels right, rather than what's logical
- expressing yourself even if you think others might not like what you have to say
- trusting your own feelings/intuition rather than doing what others suggest/expect
- trusting based on how you feel about people, rather than going by what they say/do
- strengthening your intuition by meditating, being in nature, playing music, etc
- building self-trust as the key to attracting trust in all your dealings with others.

If you trust yourself in all that you do,
your life will be transformed.

T trust
& transformation

transformation

a metamorphosis in the appearance, form and/or nature of someone or something; a complete or major change/shift in someone's outlook, values, beliefs, focus and/or direction in life

Why is it important?

- Transformation involves making fundamental changes that enhance our lives.
- It's about re-assessing our beliefs and values—and living accordingly.
- It's also about understanding the power we have to create what we want.
- There are few things more rewarding in life than self-discovery and empowerment.
- Transforming the way we perceive ourselves transforms the way we see our world.
- When we cultivate self-awareness, we find more meaning and fulfillment in life.
- We find practical ways to take charge of our circumstances, relationships, etc.
- We also begin to understand the purpose and benefit of our challenges.
- If we can transform our negative beliefs, we set ourselves free to live powerfully.

When we transform ourselves from the inside out, we change far more than ourselves.

What's the problem?

- Many of us resist/are afraid of change, even if our current situation is very unpleasant.
- We're often taught that we're victims of circumstance, with no control over our lives.
- Without the tools/understanding for self-transformation, we try to cope with things.
- We don't realize that our circumstances are a reflection of our subconscious beliefs.
- Our circumstances confirm the validity of what we believe, which keeps us stuck.
- Collective religious/social beliefs keep feeding our fears and self-doubts.
- It takes courage to break away from our accepted reality to try something new.

Resisting change means
resisting our creativity, growth and fulfillment.

How can you fix it?

You can promote the process of personal transformation by:

- questioning everything you do and why you do it
- exploring your beliefs and determining which ones serve/don't serve you
- filling in your missing pieces so you upgrade your circumstances/self-worth
- refusing to engage in negative thoughts, words, behaviour or conversations
- taking action in accordance with what you want to believe in
- mixing with positive-minded people seeking positive change and empowerment
- envisioning and imagining your goals being fulfilled and your dreams realized
- meditating and being in nature so you can integrate the changes you make
- positively affirming the power you have to create what you want
- focusing on changing yourself, since that's what changes your world.

The power to change is in your mind;
the reason for doing it is in your spirit;
and the passion for achieving it is in your heart.

U

unity
& uniqueness

unity

*the state of being united/joined as a whole; harmony or agreement between people or groups [**or within one's self**]; the quality/state of oneness*

Why is it important?

- When we feel a sense of oneness with others, we can have a meaningful connection.
- Being in harmony with others creates a sense of inner peace.
- Doing things in unison is usually more powerful than doing them alone.
- Having a shared vision, focus and direction creates synergy and purpose.
- Joining/collaborating with others motivates us to stay on track—and is more fun.
- We feel validated and appreciated if we work as part of a harmonious team.
- Working in harmony with others cultivates greater cohesion and fulfillment.
- Having a common goal/unifying purpose brings people together in meaningful ways.

By cultivating harmony within,
we attract it in those around us.

What's the problem

- Life is so hectic for many that they never experience harmony or peace of mind.
- People often don't believe that true peace or fulfillment is attainable.
- They may therefore sabotage their or others' efforts to make a difference.
- Negativity and a lack of vision can create disharmony and conflict.
- Egos/power struggles/hidden agendas tend to undermine any efforts to collaborate.
- If our own lives are lacking, we may find it hard to devote time and energy to others.
- Bringing others together requires committed, inspiring leadership.

When we live in harmony with our values and desires, everything works.

How can you fix it?

You can cultivate a greater sense of unity by:

- sharing your creative thoughts and ideas with others
- acknowledging and exploring any disharmony or conflict in your life
- being emotionally available and generous to create deeper connections
- seeking to understand any internal conflicts (the real source of external ones)
- practising yoga or other ways to be at one/in harmony with yourself
- listening to others and being open to new ways of collaborating
- being open to the insights of others, especially those relating to your contribution
- being considerate of, and staying focused on, the greater good
- realizing that there's no need to compete as your contribution is unique.

*In collaborating with others,
you can more clearly see your similarities
and more fully appreciate your uniqueness.*

U unity & uniqueness

uniqueness

being the only one of its kind; without equal or equivalent; unparalleled

Why is it important?

- Our individual uniqueness is what sets us apart and makes us distinctive.
- Our unique voice, manner, looks and personality are what make us interesting.
- Valuing and expressing our uniqueness brings far more fulfillment than trying to fit in.
- Staying true to ourselves and to who we really are is the key to happiness.
- There's little reward in trying to be like someone else–and no competitive edge.
- Our uniqueness enables us to make a difference/impact that no one else can make.
- Being uniquely, powerfully ourselves is the biggest gift we can give to our world.
- When we express and live our uniqueness, we attract our perfect partner.
- We also connect with our unique purpose, creativity and passions in life.

We thrive
when we explore, express and enjoy our uniqueness.

What's the problem?

- We are generally taught to fit in rather than cherishing our unique qualities.
- We are often afraid to do outrageous things or express our unique flair/creativity.
- We may fear that our quirky thoughts or ideas will be rejected by others.
- If we are different, we may feel that we'll end up being alone/lonely.
- In our upbringing, we're often taught to do/say the 'right' thing to fit in.
- In most education systems, we're not encouraged to explore our uniqueness.
- In seeking acceptance from others, we forget that self-acceptance comes first.

If you're not being uniquely you,
then someone, somewhere, is missing out.

How can you fix it?

You can explore and express your uniqueness by:

- being true to your unique personality, humour and values
- experimenting with the way you dress and express yourself
- trying something new–a new language, cuisine, fashion, creative activity
- spicing up your home/office environment to reflect your taste and style
- exploring and boldly expressing your ideas through writing/speaking
- not making polite conversation just for the sake of it
- making a point of saying what you mean and meaning what you say
- sharing your ideas and opinions with others
- experimenting with words/expressions that are unique to you/your way of thinking.

Being uniquely you
is the best kind of freedom that money cannot buy.

V validation
& vision

validation

support or corroboration of the value of something or someone; the recognition, illustration, confirmation or official sanction of someone's worthiness or legitimacy

Why is it important?

- Validating ourselves and being positive about who/what we are enhances self-worth.
- Acknowledging our value is an important part of creating/attracting what we want.
- Validating self is an important way of saying YES to being worthy and being loved.
- Validating others is a way of supporting and acknowledging their thoughts/feelings.
- It's also an expression of love and sensitivity for who they are.
- It shows that we are aware of, and grateful for, the unique contribution they make.
- Validation promotes understanding and more effective communication.
- It fosters healthy team work and a greater sense of community/connection.
- By validating ourselves, in healthy ways, we can cancel out any negative programming.

*We only ever need validation from others
if we haven't given it to ourselves.*

What's the problem?

- If we had critical parents/teachers, we usually end up invalidating ourselves.
- We pick up where our early 'programmers' left off–continuing their negativity.
- When we lack self-worth, we fail to recognize or acknowledge our achievements.
- If we lack confidence/self-acceptance, we may belittle our achievements or value.
- If we fail to validate ourselves in healthy ways, we cancel out our lovability.
- Self-rejection, in any form, prevents others/the universe from loving/supporting us.

How can anyone recognize you
if you're not being you?

How can you fix it?

You can cultivate validation of self and others by:

- validating yourself whenever you do something positive or challenging
- focusing on what you have already achieved rather than focusing on any shortfall
- making a point of acknowledging others for their gifts/wisdom/contribution/presence
- thinking/expressing positive thoughts about self/others, vs putting you/them down
- accepting compliments graciously and allowing others to validate you
- validating others so this quality becomes a natural part of you, inside and out
- being gentle with yourself if you make a mistake, knowing you did your best
- validating yourself if you are unjustly criticized or blamed for something you didn't do
- remembering that validating self, in healthy ways, generates validation from others.

Validating yourself brings the recognition you want,
which helps to clarify your vision of who you really are.

V validation & vision

vision

*something you imagine—a picture you see in your mind [**of your path/dreams in life**]; an experience in which a person/thing appears vividly in the mind; an imaginative anticipation*

Why is it important?

- Having a vision motivates us to do what's required to realize our dreams.
- When we have a clear vision of what we want, we're much more likely to get it.
- If we have a clear vision of our value/contribution, we attract the ideal clients/partners.
- Without a clear vision of where we're going, we may feel lost or aimless in life.
- A clear vision keeps us focused and on track, improving productivity and efficiency.
- Having a clear vision of our goals promotes enthusiasm and commitment.
- A clearly communicated, values-based vision inspires others to come on board.
- Focusing our energies/commitment on our vision mobilizes the universe to assist us.

Your vision is your own personal preview of coming attractions.

What's the problem?

- If we don't believe we're in charge of our own lives, we're unlikely to have a vision.
- We tend to focus on managing situations rather than envisioning our ideal life.
- Having a vision implies having a sense of purpose, which many people lack.
- If our dreams seem unrealistic, we're unlikely to envision realizing them.
- Creating/living our vision is a very personal process that can feel risky.
- We may allow fears, self-doubts or negativity to hold us back.
- It takes courage and commitment to believe in—and start acting on—our vision.

Without a vision,
we resign ourselves to a life with few surprises.

How can you fix it?

You can cultivate a clearer vision of you or your life by:

- writing down your goals and dreams, in practical terms
- breaking down your objectives into short- and longer-term actions
- positively affirming that you can create and realize your vision/dreams
- doing something creative to tap into your deeper feelings/yearnings
- asking like-minded, positive friends to help you formulate your ideas
- getting feedback from others about the strengths and passions they see in you
- staying flexible and being open to input/ideas as your vision evolves
- refusing to entertain any self-doubts, fears or negativity
- joining a mastermind or visioning group for support, inspiration and motivation
- creating a vision board that depicts your goals, desires and dream life.

When you clarify your vision,
you can start directing the movie of your life.

W worthiness & wealth

worthiness

*having great merit, character or value; honourable; of commendable excellence or merit; deserving [**of love, abundance, recognition and all the good things in life**]*

Why is it important?

- Our self-worth is the most important factor in our happiness and fulfillment.
- It determines how much love/money/ease/success/recognition we attract in life.
- Healthy self-worth generates positivity and confidence in our ability to thrive.
- Having solid self-worth is far more powerful than having credentials or qualifications.
- Actively demonstrating worthiness in our words/actions makes us magnetic.
- With healthy self-worth, we don't need others' approval and we're willing to take risks.
- We can laugh at ourselves and do not take offence if others don't like us.
- When we feel truly worthy, we are magnanimous, generous and open.

We're all in charge of our self-worth.
No one can make us unworthy
(although we might think they can).

What's the problem?

- Everyone lacks self-acceptance or self-worth, to some degree, in some area.
- Low self-worth can get handed down from generation to generation.
- We're usually taught to seek acceptance from others but not to give it to ourselves.
- Our parents often have high expectations of us, which can result in a fear of failure.
- A fear of not being good enough prevents us from loving ourselves and feeling worthy.
- There is pressure from the media/advertising to be perfect, which we can never be.
- Negative experiences/programming diminishes our sense of self-worth.

Affirming our worth is not enough;
we must actively live it and love it
to attract what we desire.

How can you fix it?

You can cultivate greater self-worth by:

- validating yourself for everything you manage to do, even if not perfectly
- validating others, too, to demonstrate confidence and positivity
- acting, walking and talking as if you ARE hugely worthy and deserving
- constantly affirming that you're worthy (despite some old negative programming)
- focusing on putting yourself first, in healthy ways, and feeling good about it
- taking actions that demonstrate worthiness, even if you don't yet feel worthy
- facing your fears/insecurities and addressing them (rather than hiding them)
- focusing on your strengths and blessings rather than past failures or pain
- allowing yourself to be seen for who you are and to be supported in being that.

Your self-worth will always be
matched by your wealth.

W worthiness & wealth

wealth

*an abundance of valuable possessions/money; the state of being rich; prosperity; an abundance or profusion of anything [**such as love, health, contentment**]*

Why is it important?

- Whereas having money may make you rich, wealth is more a state of mind or being.
- We might have lots of money but not necessarily feel wealthy.
- Being wealthy is usually associated with happiness and comfort, as well as money.
- The wealthy tend to be at ease with money; the poor often feel intimidated by it.
- The lives of those with a wealth of love, good health and friends are often the richest.
- True wealth (with health, love, happiness and fulfillment) comes from strong self-worth.
- We may have very few possessions yet feel immensely wealthy in our lives.
- Wealth is something we all have a right to have, given the abundance in our universe.
- How wealthy we are is a direct reflection of how worthy we subconsciously feel.

The more we love and appreciate what we already have, the more love and money we attract.

What's the problem?

- We're often taught that having lots of money is selfish or wrong.
- Poverty or being of simple means is often glorified (usually by the rich).
- We often justify being rich by making a point of helping others.
- Without healthy self-worth, we usually cannot keep or grow our money.
- If we feel undeserving, we may squander money or sabotage our success.
- A fear of success or failure usually prevents us from accumulating wealth.
- We often believe that having money is proof of our success or validity.

If we hold on tight to what we have,
for fear of not having enough,
we often end up not having enough.

How can you fix it?

You can cultivate greater wealth in your life by:

- focusing on the good things in your life, not on what's missing or deficient
- validating yourself to enhance your self-worth and self-acceptance
- exploring and resolving any fears you may have around success or wealth
- taking risks rather than living in fear or self-doubt about what's possible
- taking action rather than always thinking about/planning what you'll do
- donating/letting go of whatever you don't need, rather than hoarding things
- mixing with those who have a mentality of easy abundance and wealth
- sharing what you have with others, as do those who have plenty
- letting go of competitiveness, ideas of loss/struggle or win-lose thinking
- affirming your worthiness, magnetism and trust in self/the universe to provide.

When you demonstrate worthiness, you act wealthy;
and when you act wealthy,
the universe delivers the goods.

X

xanadu
& xoxo

xanadu

*a place of great beauty, luxury and contentment [**a sense of inner mystery and magic**]*

Why is it important?

- Believing in the possibility of true contentment and luxury keeps us optimistic.
- Believing in our own magical abilities makes us unstoppable.
- If we strive to realize our dreams, we can do amazing things along the way.
- The more we access and understand our deeper selves, the more magic we can create.
- If we hold out for our ultimate vision of what's possible, we aim higher.
- The higher we aim, the more likely we are to achieve something amazing.
- We can create our own personal xanadu, from the inside out.
- It's determined by the choices we make and how powerful we believe we are.

Even just believing in our ability to create magic in our lives makes our lives more magical.

What's the problem?

- We don't usually believe in magic—particularly in ourselves.
- We're taught that dreams of some wonderful, ultimate life are unachievable.
- Luxury and riches seem unattainable and we learn to settle for what we have.
- We're often taught that life is about working hard and fighting for our success.
- We're not usually taught that we deserve to easily achieve what we want.
- We're afraid to be too idealistic or to aim too high, for fear of disappointment.
- People around us often have negative expectations about what's possible.
- We may not find much support from others in the pursuit of our ideal life.

*If we don't believe in our right to an idyllic life,
we won't even try to find it.*

How can you fix it?

You can work towards creating your own personal xanadu by:

- visualizing your ideal life and feeling/vividly imagining all the details
- meditating to help you stay positive and focused on your dream
- being kind to yourself and taking time out, to promote your personal magnetism
- positively and enthusiastically affirming your goals and dreams as a reality
- taking positive action towards making your dream life a reality
- surrounding yourself with positive images and reminders about your xanadu
- avoiding all negativity about your ability to create magic in your life
- acting and living as if you can—and do—create magic in your life.

*When you cultivate your own personal xanadu inside
you, the universe moves to match it on the outside.*

X

xanadu
& xoxo

XOXO

hugs and kisses, typically to express affection or good friendship at the end of an exchange

Why is it important?

- Love and affection are two of the most powerful and life-affirming qualities we have.
- As children, we need love and affection in order to thrive and feel secure in our world.
- As adults, our ability to love/show affection is vital for healthy, loving relationships.
- Love, affection and friendship also keep us happy, healthy and positive about life.
- Expressing our love and affection for others builds connection and harmony.
- The more love and friendship we share with others, the more loving our world becomes.
- As we increasingly work/play/connect online, we need love and affection all the more.
- Reaching out to others with affection/friendship helps prevent bullying and loneliness.
- It can help pull someone (including you) out of depression—and can even save lives.

Heartfelt hugs and affection
can often comfort us more than advice or wise words.

What's the problem?

- True love and affection are rare, for many, as we live such busy, fragmented lives.
- As we work/communicate more online, we're often deprived of touch/love/friendship.
- Many young people, especially, are feeling isolated, unloved and disconnected.
- Parents often focus on their children's achievements, rather than expressing affection.
- Grades and performance are often considered more important than issues of the heart.
- If our parents lacked love/affection, growing up, they may have difficulty expressing it.
- Many people feel shy or nervous about openly expressing affection or warmth.
- Fear of rejection or ridicule often keeps people from reaching out to others.

If we're closed off to affection and friendship,
we're not open to being liked or loved.

How can you fix it?

You can cultivate more affection and friendship by:

- reaching out to those who seem lonely/isolated—at work, school, etc
- taking every opportunity to express your affection and caring for loved ones
- staying in contact with friends and making time to meet up in person
- inviting people to dinner for meaningful sharing and intimate conversation
- remembering the power and value of small gestures—cards, flowers, small gifts
- saying what you feel, rather than pretending to be tough or that you don't care
- joining a men's/women's group to offer and receive support and friendship
- giving others the benefit of the doubt, rather than jumping to negative conclusions
- reaching out to others, rather than waiting for them to make the first move
- being especially warm and friendly to those who seem least able to reciprocate.

Never underestimate the power of your affection
on those whose hearts seem most hardened.

Y youthfulness & yes!

youthfulness

*the dynamism, vitality, appearance, freshness, spirit and/or exuberance characteristic of one who is young [**a state of mind born of optimism, curiosity and trust in self**]*

Why is it important?

- Being young at heart, even if not in body, is vital to our continued well-being.
- Maintaining a mentality of youthfulness keeps us engaged in—and positive about—life.
- Cultivating a youthful spirit and attitude helps keep us young and energized.
- The longer we maintain our youthfulness, the more we can contribute to others.
- Staying young in spirit also keeps us connected to the younger generation.
- With youthfulness, we are open, curious and interested in the world around us.
- When we keep ourselves young, we are more independent and self-sufficient.
- We are fun to be with when we stay vital, dynamic and engaged in life.

Aging is all in the mind,
so make up your mind to stay young.

What's the problem?

- Stress and competing priorities at work/home can deplete our reserves.
- Chronic stress ages us, hastening physical degeneration and sapping us of our drive.
- We fear aging and being side-lined by society, which prevents us from fully living.
- The very young/elderly tend to be stereotyped, rather than being seen as individuals.
- In the media, too much focus is placed on looking rather than acting youthful.
- We forget that part of youthfulness is about playing and being creative.
- If we don't feel excited about life, we tend to feel less youthful and vital.

When you cultivate a beginner's mind,
you start each day fresh, with curiosity and no regrets.

How can you fix it?

You can generate more youthfulness by:

- continuing to explore and learn new things, which generates new brain cells
- befriending/mentoring a young person, so you benefit from each other's perspective
- staying active so that the body and the mind remain vital and energized
- travelling to new places to keep expanding your horizons and outlook
- savouring the good things in life (such as wine and chocolate), in moderation
- talking to those much younger/older than you, rather than labelling/avoiding them
- dressing 'young' and having fun with clothes, versus dressing your age
- cultivating dynamic friendships with plenty of fun and laughter time
- maintaining your own unique style and flair, rather than holding on to old stuff
- taking power naps and meditating, to de-stress and focus on what matters in life.

The most powerful way to stay youthful
is to keep saying YES! to life.

Y

youthfulness
& yes!

yes!

used to express affirmation, agreement, positive affirmation or consent [expressing openness and receptivity to things]

Why is it important?

- Being open and receptive to life makes us much warmer, nicer people.
- We're more likely to manifest what we need when we're open to new possibilities.
- Saying Yes! to love/life opens doors and gives the universe permission to support us.
- It means we're open to loving and being loved, and we trust that things will work out.
- It also demonstrates healthy self-worth/acceptance, which enhances our magnetism.
- Being positive generates positivity and enthusiasm in others.
- Saying Yes! means we're willing to take risks and to be adventurous.
- Our finances, relationships and life experiences all improve when we're receptive.
- Being positive generates vitality, opens our minds and expands our horizons.
- Problems are not problems when we're open to things working out positively.

Negative thinking is just as powerful as positive thinking, but not half as much fun.

What's the problem?

- If we've been taught that life is hard, we often expect the worst to happen.
- We may consider taking risks to be too risky, due to a fear of failure.
- We often don't trust ourselves or believe that we can make things work.
- Disappointments may lead us to believe that things don't usually go our way.
- If we've had a difficult upbringing, we may see our world as a scary, unfriendly place.
- If we focus on problems or challenges, all the good stuff becomes blurry.
- Misery loves company; mixing with negative people can feed our fears.

The more you say YES to what is,
the more receptive you are to what could be.

How can you fix it?

You can start saying YES to more life by:

- watching your words and expressing things as positively as possible
- ensuring that your reasons for saying NO to something are not fear-based
- identifying and revitalizing any areas of your life that are stagnant or stale
- allowing yourself to be supported, helped or mentored by others
- consciously saying YES to something that's scary but potentially good for you
- daring to show up/contribute more—being a speaker, doing a workshop etc
- heeding your body and saying YES to meeting its needs, healthily, in the moment
- opening up to deeper intimacy or connection in relationships
- saying YES to every day, every moment and every opportunity
- seeing everything as a YES; even a NO to something unworkable is a YES to you!

YES is your personal invitation to life.

Z

zen
& zero

zen

*mindful awareness and presence; a state of mind based on peaceful detachment [**the ability to live without reactivity or angst**]*

Why is it important?

- Being present frees us from the regrets of the past and the fears of the future.
- The ability to be Zen-like brings us emotional freedom and serenity.
- We understand that there is no rush or need to arrive at some future moment.
- When we practise a Zen-like state of mind, we let go of stress and anxiety.
- We create a state in which we are open and receptive to life and love.
- Only when we are present and calm can we be connected to our true selves.
- When we are present and aware, we receive insights, inspiration and guidance.
- We stay connected to what matters in life and our choices become clear.

*Zen-ness is something that resides within,
not 'out there' in some workshop or monastery.*

What's the problem?

- We are constantly distracted by electronic gadgets and fast-paced living.

- When we multi-task, we cannot focus fully on what we're doing.

- We are usually surrounded by noise, activity and demands from others.

- If we feel anxious or overwhelmed, we may not take time to meditate.

- When we are busy or stressed, we find it hard to switch off and be present.

- Achieving a Zen-like state is most difficult when we most need to do it.

- We're spiritual beings in need of peace/serenity, yet we often neglect our spirit.

*Being Zen is not something you do;
it's something you realize.*

How can you fix it?

You can become more Zen-like by:

- doing things more slowly, with focus and concentration

- doing only one thing at a time—and doing it fully and well

- being mindful of your breath and movements as you go about your day

- doing fewer things, to avoid multi-tasking or fragmenting your focus

- being mindful and aware of everything you do, with all of your senses

- taking things in, rather than walking around with your mind elsewhere

- designating time every day to sitting quietly and meditating

- eliminating unnecessary things from your life and your schedule

- accepting what is, rather than wasting energy on things that cannot be changed.

*When you reclaim your natural Zen-ness,
you take yourself back to 'ground zero'.*

Z
zen
& zero

zero

*a state of neutrality; the starting point of something [**back to the beginning or origins of something—such as you**]*

Why is it important?

- Hitting the 'reset' button in our hearts and minds brings us back to our centre.
- Reclaiming our original blueprint puts us back in touch with who we really are.
- When we reconnect with our original self, life works so much better.
- Coming back to zero means letting go of all the stuff we've taken on from others.
- It means being authentically ourselves and not living by other people's rules.
- Shedding limiting beliefs/letting go of our negative mental programming sets us free.
- Mastering the art of detachment and neutrality brings a sense of peace and calm.
- When we zero in on what really matters to us, we gain a healthier perspective.
- If we strip away the busyness/frenzy of modern life, we reconnect with our power.

Forget about going from zero to hero;
you'll feel like a hero when you get back to zero.

What's the problem?

- We may catch glimpses of our deeper selves, but find it hard to stay connected.
- Staying true to ourselves is almost impossible in our stressful, fast-paced world.
- Early programming, the media and religions distort our sense of self.
- Due to these external influences, we are largely out of touch with our power.
- We are distracted by gadgets, technology and multi-tasking lifestyles
- We tend to think of zero as being a place of nothingness, rather than peace.
- We are so busy trying to get somewhere that we have difficulty just being.

The original you is flawless and fantastic;
to reclaim your true self,
your mind must be lawless and elastic.

How can you fix it?

You can take yourself back to your own 'ground zero' by:

- assessing your beliefs to determine which ones really serve you
- consciously letting go of limiting beliefs/fears/worry/others' expectations
- mindfully identifying the reasons for your choices/actions/inaction
- filling in your missing pieces so that you come home to your true self
- not pre-judging people/situations before fully processing them
- letting go of reactivity and focusing instead on finding the deeper truth
- removing any negative 'labels' that you've attached to yourself and others
- discarding old habits/routines in favour of authenticity and new choices
- emptying your mind and returning to simplicity and stillness.

When you dig deeply to unearth your original blueprint,
you tap into the richest natural elements on Earth.

Key points to remember

Find out about your negative subconscious beliefs so that they no longer run your life. When it is negatively programmed, your subconscious mind can be the biggest saboteur of your relationships; with a little positive, conscious collaboration, it can become your most powerful ally in creating what you want.

Fill in your 'missing pieces' and you will automatically attract a partner with those same qualities. Your 'missing pieces' (e.g., acceptance, trust, respect, validation), will cause you to attract a partner with the same 'missing pieces' as you, which means you will only ever get what you want when you fill in these missing elements in yourself. Filling in your missing pieces automatically brings you the fullness of life you've been seeking.

Dare to do and say what feels right for you, rather than trying to conform. We tend to distort ourselves in order to be acceptable, hiding our opinions and often suppressing our unique personality. But not being authentic means that we cannot attract what we want in life because we are not being true to ourselves. When we are authentic, we attract partners and situations that reflect and share our values.

Remember that emotional pain is the result of a conflict between what you want (such as love, acceptance, recognition) and what you are actually getting. If you are in pain in your relationship, it's almost certainly due to a belief that you're unlovable or not good enough, which is keeping you stuck. Find out what's going on inside and you'll find the key to resolving your pain.

Start looking at your relationships as the key to your success and fulfillment. Relationships are designed to take you on a journey of self-discovery, healing and empowerment, and they are never random or accidental. Each partner you attract is there to show you what is missing within you, what you subconsciously believe about yourself, and what you need to do in order to enhance your self-worth. The answers are inside you; the clues to finding them are in your relationships.

12 principles of empowerment

(which can also be used as powerful, positive, daily affirmations)

1. When I transform my negative programming, I can create what I want.

2. When I fill in my missing pieces, I attract a partner who is similarly complete.

3. My self-worth determines how much love, money, success, ease and fulfillment I have in my life.

4. Saying NO to what doesn't work for me automatically attracts something better.

5. Problems, challenges and 'difficult' people are in my life so that I can discover who I am and grow strong in certain areas.

6. My programming/missing pieces represent the flip side of my greatest strengths.

7. True intimacy, connection and happiness come from being authentically me.

8. Circumstances are a direct reflection of what I subconsciously think about me.

9. When I connect with myself and fully express who I am, magic happens.

10. The more I take care of me, in healthy ways, the more I am taken care of.

11. When I operate from the inside out, the world responds to me.

12. Trusting my intuition takes me where I am meant to go.

About the author

Olga Sheean is an empowerment coach specializing in relationships, human dynamics and holistic self-mastery. She provides individual, group and corporate training in how to maximize personal and professional performance, while enhancing leadership, creativity and magnetism. Working from the inside out, Olga teaches powerful techniques for transforming negative subconscious programming and achieving greater ease, success and fulfillment.

Over the past 25 years, Olga has worked internationally as a coach, counsellor, writer, magazine/book editor, publisher and photo-journalist. She offers consultations, empowerment intensives, relationship workshops, corporate coaching, Dream Teams©, Life Changers©, practitioner training and customized online training worldwide.

She is the author of *Fit for Love–find your self and your perfect mate*; *Gut Feelings–the inside story*; and *DiscoverYou–an e-course in self-mastery*.

For more information: www.olgasheean.com /olga@olgasheean.com

www.ingramcontent.com/pod-product-compliance
Lightning Source LLC
Chambersburg PA
CBHW060118050426
42448CB00010B/1933